Also by Era Zistel

Treasury of Cat Stories
Golden Book of Cat Stories
Golden Book of Dog Stories
Orphan
The Good Year
Wintertime Cat
The Gentle People
Thistle
The Dangerous Year
Hi Fella
Good Companions

THISTLE & CO.

THISTLE & CO.

Era Zistel

With Photographs by the Author

Little, Brown and Company—Boston–Toronto

FIRST EDITION

LIBRARY OF CONGRESS CATALOGING IN PUBLICATION DATA

Zistel, Era.
Thistle & Co.

1. Raccoons as pets—Anecdotes, facetiae, satire, etc. 2. Skunks as pets—Anecdotes, facetiae, satire, etc. 3. Raccoons—Anecdotes. 4. Skunks—Anecdotes. 5. Cats—Anecdotes. 6. Zistel, Era. I. Title.
SF416.Z57 1982 818'.5407 81-15611
ISBN 0-316-98798-0 AACR2

MV
Designed by Susan Windheim
Published simultaneously in Canada
by Little, Brown & Company (Canada) Limited

PRINTED IN THE UNITED STATES OF AMERICA

For Anne Marie,
who has been faithful
in her fashion

THISTLE & CO.

1

YOU COULD SAY that it all began with Thistle.

From experience I had learned that if a stranger knocking on my door didn't have something clutched in his hand or cradled in his arms, there'd almost certainly be a box containing a mystery sitting next to his feet.

This man was holding against his chest a small piece of soggy brown fur that turned out to be an infant raccoon, found, he said, in a rain-soaked ditch at the side of the road. The limp body looked so close to death that there didn't seem to be much hope, but I told the man I'd see what I could do. With the little thing wrapped in a blanket, I gave her the customary dose of penicillin, then, after she had revived somewhat, persuaded her to suck a bit of bread soaked in milk, from the palm of my hand.

Two days later she was happily making messes by

paddling in the bread and milk, and clinging to me so tenaciously that I found it almost impossible to get free. I'd pull off one burrlike paw, and find it stuck tight to me again after I had managed to unfasten a second one. That was why she was named Thistle.

Her eyes were still light baby blue, indicating that she was no more than a couple of weeks old, but she gained strength so rapidly that in no time she was crawling all over me, letting me know when she was hungry, which was almost constantly, by sucking on whatever part of me happened to be handiest, my arm, my neck, my cheek, an ear. And whenever I tried to leave her she didn't just cry. She shrieked as if she were being murdered.

Racoons are among the most gregarious of all animals. It's not unusual for ten or more to be living together. Youngsters remain with their mothers from the time they are born until the following spring, or until, at the age of two, they are ready to have offspring of their own. Even then, if living quarters are roomy enough — abandoned buildings being favored — they will stay on, much to the bewilderment of the different sets of babies, who will attach themselves to whichever mother happens to be nearest, only to be fiercely repulsed if it's the wrong one.

By some mischance, then, Thistle had lost not only her mother but also an indeterminate number of brothers, sisters, cousins, and aunts, and was so desperately lonely that it seemed even the hostility of the cats in the house would be better for her than no companionship at all. So I lifted her out of the cardboard box filled with hay and put her down in the larger territory occupied by the cats.

Having shared the house on various other occasions with opossums, squirrels, wood rats, chipmunks, birds, and once, briefly, a fox, the cats had achieved a certain amount of tolerance for other species. Moreover, since they themselves, most of them, were foundlings, they had something in common with Thistle, although it was most unlikely that they were aware of this affinity.

The three Inkspots had been found in a box left lying on the road. Mercy, so named because the little boys who had brought her had pleaded so eloquently that she be given a home, had had a like origin. Cleo had been transported some two hundred miles from Albany, where she had been snatched from almost certain death on a busy street. Mamma Mia, who became just plain Mia after a visit to the vet, had been discovered in the woods, trying to raise a family unaided, and Paddy and Pert were the two of her progeny that survived. Only Marco, who at an early age had been blinded by an encounter with an automobile, and Cricket, the mother cat, were, so to speak, legitimate, having been properly born in the house in which they lived. Perhaps that was why they felt somewhat more secure. While all the other cats heaved a collective sigh and prudently removed themselves from Thistle's immediate vicinity, Marco, who couldn't see this latest arrival anyway, remained stolidly hunched on his favorite chair of the moment, and Cricket continued her mothering, placidly allowing her four-week-old kitten to chew on one of her ears.

When I was a little girl I had an Aunt Minnie who constantly fussed over me. Her name wasn't really Minnie, but Wilhelmina probably was too much of a mouthful for her and other young members of the family, so by the time I came along nobody remembered her as anything but Minnie. She had two children of her own but must have had a lot of mothering left over, because like a broody hen she was constantly clucking over me, worrying about whether I was properly dressed, properly fed, properly supervised, and protected from harm.

Cricket was so much the same that I often called her Aunt Minnie. Always on the alert, she would be immediately in attendance to defend, console, or administer to any member of the family, no matter of what age or size. If I inadvertently stepped on someone's tail, thus provoking a surprised hiss, I had to apologize not only to the injured party but also, even more profusely, to her. Any sort of disagreement between two or more members of the family never got very far, because no matter where it took place or where she happened to be, she intervened so swiftly and with such authority that the disputants settled the argument at once by retreating in opposite directions. The runt of her litter, so small that even in adulthood she looked like no more than a half-grown kitten, she nevertheless was the indomitable Matriarch, the all-embracing Mother.

So here was Thistle, a miserable little creature, strange in appearance and somewhat obnoxious in odor, but sorely in need of mothering. Grunting an invitation, Cricket rolled on her side to offer her milk, but it seemed her spigots were not like a raccoon's. Thistle either couldn't find them or couldn't figure out how they worked. However, Cricket became at least half a mother. I, provider of food, was the other half. When Thistle was hungry she came to me. When she was frightened, she went to hide as best she could behind the diminutive Cricket.

Cricket's single kitten, named Chowder because he was a little bit of everything including Manx, with only a stub of a tail to wiggle, was both curious and wary of Thistle. Abandoning his pastime of chewing on his mother's ear, he circled around to sniff cautiously at the newcomer's rear, where in almost all animals but man identity is established, and immediately was diverted by the entrancingly bushy tail.

Fortunately raccoons are blessed with pelts so dense as to be almost impenetrable. Thistle didn't mind having her tail mauled. In fact she responded so affably that soon she and Chowder were tumbling about in clumsy kitten games, while Cricket sat with paws primly tucked under her, watching with apparent approval. And when she retired that night she had two youngsters nestled against her belly, one of which she washed industriously for a long time, to try to make it smell more like a cat.

Thistle soon became convinced that she was indeed a cat. With older members of the family her socializing consisted mainly of teasing if she could get away with it, pouncing on a tail when the owner wasn't looking, or confronting a napping cat with a view of her capacious mouth that seemed to promise a sudden demise. But her relationship with Chowder was one of sibling affection. They played together by the hour, chasing each other across a room and back again, climbing up on chairs and down, tumbling in and out of cardboard boxes, until, suddenly exhausted, they curled up in one of the boxes and fell instantly asleep, and sometimes Cricket joined them there, if she could manage to squeeze in.

So that I wouldn't have to be in constant attendance, I had turned one panel of a screen door into a little swinging door, and when Chowder accidentally pushed against it he was fascinated to discover that it led outside. For a while he was content just to slip in and out, while Thistle watched. Then he lost his footing and tumbled down the steps, and of course Thistle had to follow.

Chowder bounced after a windblown leaf. Full of fear, Thistle tobogganed down the steps to join him, and soon pursuit of the leaf turned into a game of chasing each other around a hemlock tree, until Chowder abandoned that diversion to whisk up the trunk.

Grown raccoons are as much at home in trees as on the ground, but young ones evidently must be instructed in the art of climbing, somewhat the way ducklings have to be taught to swim. While Chowder capered among the branches, Thistle slowly hauled her more bulky body up the trunk. Mischievously Chowder lured her to the very top, then with feline agility slipped past her and skinned on down, leaving her utterly forlorn. Slumped in a crotch, she whimpered in terror, and of course that brought Cricket to the rescue.

Cricket was afraid of trees. Never had she tried going up one more than a couple of feet, then had descended with as much trepidation as if she were climbing down Mt. Everest. But she was a mother. When offspring are in danger, mothers are fearless. With a fine show of bravery she climbed all the way to the crotch where Thistle cowered, then with little reassuring grunts showed her how to back down, but with such fear of her own that she could hardly transfer from one shaking paw to the other. Obediently Thistle followed, headfirst, and soon discovered she could wrap her stubby legs around the trunk to dig her long claws in like crampons. By the time she reached the ground, she had grown so confident that just to prove scaling a tree was no great feat she clambered back up, while Cricket watched in dismay.

Meanwhile, Chowder had gone exploring around the side of the house, and had just discovered the pool when Thistle caught up with him. Both of them were already acquainted with water to some extent. Thistle had had great fun playing with a dripping faucet in the bathtub, which from then on was profusely decorated with her footprints, and Chowder had got more than one soaking when Thistle plugged the faucet with a paw, then gleefully released the water to spray it over everything, including a fleeing Chowder.

But so large a body of water as the pool demanded respect. Chowder prowled around the bank, taking care not to get too near, while Thistle went into a typical raccoon shuffle of indecision, approaching and retreating, until finally she dipped her paws into the water, then ran like mad to hide behind Cricket.

Raccoons fortunate enough to live near a body of water may spend considerable time in it, catching fish, searching for edibles in the shallows. Their reputation for washing food seems quite unfounded, but they do delight in dunking what they don't want to eat, or what they consider refuse, vigorously sloshing it up and down like peasant women doing laundry in a stream. They are excellent swimmers, and sometimes take refuge in deep water to escape from pursuers. Many a tale has been told of raccoons luring pursuing dogs into deep water, then diving underneath to rip open their bellies.

It was essential, then, for Thistle to become acquainted with the pool, but parental guidance seemed to be needed for this venture as well as for tree climbing, so I took off my shoes and socks and waded into the water. Chowder at once found something to do elsewhere, but for Thistle I was still half a mother. With little snuffles of mistrust, she followed me into this strange element, wading in gingerly, until in deeper water the wading changed to paddling, and so she learned to swim. Her passage, with only the top of her head showing, was so smooth that it caused not the slightest ripple, and it was lovely to watch. At the far side of the pool, she found shallow water in a miniature cave under a big boulder, and spent some time there feeling along the floor with busy hands, searching for she couldn't have known what. Her teeth were still small, her diet mostly bread and milk and canned cat food. But one day those nimble, groping fingers would be adept at locating crayfish, hellgrammites, worms, water bugs, eggs, and larvae.

She and Chowder began to differ in other ways, too. Whenever we had visitors, Chowder turned shy and slipped out of sight, while Thistle greeted everyone with enthusiasm. She had a great love for people that unfortunately was seldom reciprocated, at least by grown-ups. After having their ankles nipped, their legs climbed, their fingers chewed, their watches removed, their ears and nostrils explored, their hair searched for fleas, most found excuses for a hasty departure, for which, in some cases, I gave fervent thanks concealed under profuse apologies.

Youngsters were more tolerant. They yipped and yelped, giggled and groaned, but all in all had a perfectly marvelous time submitting to Thistle's mauling. Yet much as she enjoyed these side attractions, Chowder remained her most loved playmate, and at the end of each strenuous day he was always her sleeping companion. Lying snuggled against him or curled around him, overflowing to conceal his body almost entirely, she purred for a while, then puffed and snorted through a repetition of the day's activities in a dream.

They were inseparable, and they had to be separated. Shortly after his birth, Chowder had been promised to a friend, and the time came for him to go to his new home. One moment he was there with Thistle, the next moment he was unaccountably gone. She couldn't believe in his absence, couldn't understand my inability to find him for her, rejected with impatience, even outbursts of fury, my attempts to console her. All through the house she searched for him, peering behind doors and under furniture and in corners, then looked all around outside, even up in the branches of their favorite tree. With little trills of invitation and inquiry she called out to him, until at last she gave up and slumped in a corner, head bowed, her usually busy hands resting on her belly like a tired old peasant woman's.

The unexpected show of grief distressed me so that I'd have asked for Chowder's return, if that had been possible. But he had been taken far away, halfway across the continent.

Finally she emerged from desolation to become attached to a rag — actually a pair of my panties filched from the laundry and properly torn — which she carried with her everywhere, like a child's security blanket. Lying on her back, she hugged it to her, patted it lovingly, and pulled it over her, stretch-it in all sorts of ghostly shapes. Or, putting it aside for a while, she had a quiet game with one of my sneakers, the one for the right foot. No other shoe would do, not even this one's mate. If in tidying up I put it away, or she forgot where she had left it, she went around trilling complaints and begging, until I dropped whatever I was doing and helped her hunt for it. With these two surrogate companions, the rag and the shoe, she managed to keep busy for hours, but she was far from happy. They were poor substitutes for Chowder.

As if taking pity on her, Cricket produced another kitten, and Thistle was entranced. Arching her big body over the little thing, she tried to entice it into a game, but it was entirely too small and helpless. Besides, Cricket's disposition had become unpredictable. One moment she was friendly enough, watching Thistle's clumsy attempts to play with apparent approval. Then without warning she would growl and hiss, sending Thistle off to sag again in a corner, like a done-in bag lady.

It was time for her to leave, too, for a more normal life in the woods. Day after day I took her out walking with me, and to some extent she enjoyed the excursions, stopping occasionally to examine this and that, mostly by patting with her hands, but actually showing little interest in our surroundings, and making no attempt to climb trees. If a dog barked not far away she remained unperturbed, proving that as half a mother I was a failure. I should have been teaching her how to be cautious and fearful, and hadn't the slightest idea of how to do so.

When danger threatens, or sometimes when there

is no danger but the routine is gone through something like a fire drill, a mother raccoon grunts almost like a pig. Babies soon learn to recognize these grunts as a warning, and hasten to join her in climbing up the trunk of the nearest tree. Once that lesson has been learned they are taught another. Mamma grunts a warning, but instead of taking them up the tree she stays on the ground to stand guard while they scramble up. Then, having made sure they are safe, she climbs, too, but up a different tree. This seems to be a trait found in many wild animals, mothers giving their young ones some measure of protection by calling attention to their own presence elsewhere. And somehow from this behavior of hers the raccoon babies learn another lesson, that instead of all going one way they should scatter, each going up a different tree, if there are enough in the vicinity.

The barking of a dog, the screech of an owl, the crackling of a twig under a furtive footfall, the roar of an approaching car on the road, all are sounds that mamma's grunts tell the babies may be dangerous, and so they learn not only to fear, but what they should fear.

How could I impart this knowledge to Thistle? Even if I had been able to grunt something like a pig, there was little likelihood that she would regard this as anything but another of my weird attempts at singing. So she remained blissfully ignorant and unafraid, until she learned at least one lesson the hard way.

It was on a hot, lazy day, the kind meant not for exercise but for loafing. We went a little way into the woods and I sat on a rock while Thistle puttered around nearby, fingering pebbles and twigs and patting the ground like a nearsighted person hunting for her glasses. Finally, probably out of boredom, she climbed a tall maple tree. I watched her hitching up the trunk like a lineman going up a telephone pole, heard her claws catching on the bark as she disappeared in the dense foliage above, then was startled by what sounded like a small explosion, and down she plummeted, accompanied by several shrieking baby birds and their furious mother. In what seemed like only a split second, a whole flock of birds came from nowhere, screaming and circling and diving, attacking Thistle with their beaks.

Apparently she had bumbled into a bluejay's nest, probably without knowing what it was or even that it was there, and bluejays are not only very loyal to each other but fiercely protective of their young.

I remembered that one summer a man who lived down the road had had to approach his cabin by a circuitous route because a bluejay had built her nest in a tree above his customary path, and dive-bombed him whenever he tried to pass underneath. I also remembered the fate of the crow that somehow had incurred the wrath of a flock of jays. Desperately trying to escape, the crow had flown this way and that only to be relentlessly pursued by the screaming jays, until it tired and at once was set upon, and sent fluttering to the ground. Now Thistle was in the same danger. If she tried to run she would be pursued, and unless she found cover somewhere, might be pecked to death. Shouting and clapping my hands and finally throwing stones, I managed to distract the jays long enough for me to run to her and scoop her up, and while the frustrated birds circled around the still shrieking babies, I carried her off.

Fortunately she had ducked down to protect her eyes, and the sharp beaks had not been able to penetrate her thick pelt. Except for some lacerations on the top of her head she was uninjured, but so shaken that even her teeth chattered. Safely back in the house she spent several hours in a corner, and of course that was the last time we went walking in the woods.

But after a few days of desultory playing with her rag, her shoe, and a broken cup she'd also grown fond of, she went outside with me again, just at dusk. We didn't go anywhere. I sat on the steps and she pattered around nearby, until finally she climbed a tree growing next to the house, close enough so that a big branch overhung the roof. From the branch she dropped down to rummage in the gutters and play with beechnut husks left there by the birds, and when I went indoors she didn't seem to notice. But after a while I heard her scrambling down the trunk of the tree, and she was at the door asking to be let in.

Each evening after that she went up on the roof, and the time she spent there lengthened, until she stayed the whole night. Through most of the next day she slept, awakening at sundown to have a quiet game with her rag and shoe and the broken cup, and as soon as the light faded from the sky she stood at the door asking to be let out. While I watched with approval she climbed the tree, tightrope walked along the branch, and dropped onto the roof, and I went back into the house feeling certain that I didn't have to worry about her. She was becoming a night animal, as was proper, and had found a safe place to make an adjustment to living out of doors. Surely nothing could happen to her up there on the roof.

But after a while I heard sounds of bickering, indicating that she was having a fairly serious argument with somebody. I hurried out, stood at the foot of the tree and called, and a veritable cascade of raccoons came tumbling down over the side of the roof. It looked as though all the residents in the neighborhood had come by to pay their not-too-cordial respects. After the last of them had scampered away I called again. Thistle poked her head over to peer down at me and answer with a trill. Then she disappeared, and I heard her padding about, chasing something that rolled. An hour later I went out and called again. This time she didn't appear, nor did she answer.

For two days the house was uncomfortably peaceful without her. On the third day I faced up to the likelihood that she had become a victim of a dog, or a fox, or an owl, or a car on the road, and put away her rag and shoe and the broken cup. On the fourth day I went out to search for her body, hoping I wouldn't find it but knowing perfectly well that in the vastness of the woods not finding it was no reassurance.

Then late that night, or rather early in the morning, I was awakened by a persistent pounding on the door, and when I opened it in walked Thistle with two friends, youngsters as uneasy and brash as urchins from the other side of the railroad tracks. Emboldened by her assurance, the two made a lightning inspection of the house, sending off abruptly awakened cats like rockets in all directions, paying no attention to my suggestions that they leave, until they were enticed out with an offering of cookies. Thistle hesitated for only a moment, took a cookie, and went with them.

At an earlier hour the next night she came again, this time with a whole gang of raccoons, all sizes and ages. By some means, the two visitors of the previous night must have told everybody that I was good for a handout, because they refused to depart until I gave each a slice of bread, the expenditure in cookies being prohibitive. Thistle took her slice and put it in her mouth, snatched another slice, and with considerable difficulty managed to get both outside, where she squatted with one slice hidden under her belly while she hastily consumed the other.

From then on she was no longer a raccoon in the house but an accredited member of the mob living in the woods, coming with them to participate in the nightly ritual of making a racket at the back door, and demanding tribute when it opened.

2

AT A GATHERING of people engaged in various literary pursuits, the conversation touched upon the importance of precise word selection, went on from there to an appreciation of the vast choices the English language offered, and finally to a debate over which word each of us thought was the most beautiful. After considerable pondering, the various members of the group made their selections, most of them onomatopoetic words of several syllables. When I voiced my own choice, reaction ranged from perplexity to disbelief. Beautiful? What was beautiful about a common, plain little old word like *home?*

Think, I said. Wasn't there beauty in the way such a simple utterance could lend itself to so wide a range of emotion, from the caress of familiarity to a far-away yearning, then to the joyous returning shout? Was there not beauty in the word's meaning?

What meaning?

"It has none for me," said a woman about to depart on a six-month tour of Europe.

Perhaps that is one of the things wrong with the civilization we have achieved, the reason for our disintegrating family life, the aimless drifting of our young. The cohesive, most powerful of all instincts, the love of home, has been lost. In most other species, all the way down to those we consider primitive, attachment to home exerts a force stronger than the sex drive, stronger than the need for food, stronger even than the will to survive.

I have seen a spider brushed off a wall struggle through wet paint to try to return to the web that was its home. I have seen a wood rat safely marooned on high ground plunge into flood water to swim desperately back to its inundated nest. The horse's fight to reenter the burning barn is of course legendary. But most astounding of all was my discovery that such a homing instinct apparently existed even in a lowly worm.

Spring torrents always washed quantities of silt and decaying leaves into the pools of the brook, and one of my chores in early summer was to clean out the pools and put the rich loam on what optimistically started out to be, but never became, a garden. One day as I was spreading a load of the mud, I noticed a slight undulation in it, and carefully probing with a finger, I pulled out one of those very long, thin, white worms that as children we called horsehairs, in the belief that they actually had evolved from the hairs of horses shed into the water. Never before had I seen one close up, and now I was amazed, even moved a bit, to discover that the worm had little black eyes, which in their white setting were not only very pretty but even expressive, thus elevating a primitive creature to an entity with at least a rudimentary personality. So I scooped it out of the mud and carried it, coiled in the palm of my hand, to the nearest pool, some distance from the one upstream where it had lived.

Thus I made a startling discovery. Lowered into the water, the worm stayed immobile for a while, then made quick little darts, thrusting its head from one side to another, each time pulling back as if in fear. Was it possible that the worm knew it was in a strange place? Why should the water in this pool, the same water as in the one above, seem so unfamiliar as to engender apprehension? Taking the worm back into my hand, I carried it up to the "home" pool and lowered it into the water there. Instantly it came alive and swam — happily, I presume — to a rock on the far side, under which it slithered into what probably was its lair.

My interpretation of its behavior would have seemed like foolish anthropomorphism if I hadn't read shortly afterward Robert Ardrey's account of experiments conducted with the planarian worm, a creature so primitive that it "lacks a brain, blood, sex and even a rectum." Yet after having got used to finding its food in a certain bowl, the worm came to identify this as its "home" bowl, and would pass by a number of similar bowls containing the same food, to feed always at this "home" bowl.

Further experiments made with subjects somewhat higher on the evolutionary scale established that wasps taken half a mile away from their homes returned in fifteen minutes, deer mice transported two miles from theirs managed to get back again in two days, and albatross that the U.S. Navy removed from Midway Island traveled four thousand one hundred and twenty miles in thirty-two days to return to their home territory.

What a wrenching experience the deprivation of home must be, then, for the higher forms of life — excepting, of course, man, who seems to have evolved to the point of loving not much of anything but himself. And what exquisite cruelty it is to pluck any animal out of what has become its home to toss it into some alien environment.

I had no intentions of subjecting Thistle to such a trauma, nor, indeed, was there any need to consider

Thistle meets the cats soon after her arrival, and is adopted by Cricket.

Thistle

Cricket's kitten Chowder and Thistle become constant playmates

. . . and are inseparable even when they are tired.

Thistle loves to tease the other cats, but she never teases Cricket.

Thistle quickly learns to climb trees, and is soon as much at home in a tree as on the ground.

She also learns to swim, and finds a cave under a boulder in the pool.

Thistle mourns Chowder, who has gone to a new home.

Cricket has a new kitten, but it is too little to play with . . .

so Thistle finds other things to play with.

Finally Thistle moves outside, living under the house instead of in it.

She comes back for a visit every night, bringing a lot of friends with her.

One of the friends is a skunk, named Jake. He lives under the barn.

Most of the time Jake is friendly, although sometimes he threatens with his tail.

Jake was misnamed. It turns out he is a she and a mother.

taking any action. True, because of the company she kept she was no longer welcome in the only home she'd ever known. Actually she showed little desire to return to it, except for handouts. Yet in a way it continued to be her home, with a slight adjustment. Instead of living in the house, she lived under it.

With a strength I didn't know she possessed, she managed to remove several big stones from the foundation, thus gaining access to the crawl space under the house, and for several days she worked ardently on tearing down insulation from under the flooring. Carefully shredded, it provided material for a fine nest located in a far corner, where the crawl space became too narrow for a human to enter.

When at last everything in this new location was to her liking, she had what might be called a housewarming, and from the sounds that came up through the floorboards, an extraordinary variety of snorts, shrieks, and growls, I deduced that the party was very well attended and everyone had a rousing good time.

Hollow trees are not too easy to come by, so there's a more or less perpetual housing shortage among tree dwellers in the woods. A severe windstorm results in blowdowns that might be likened to a disastrous fire in a city tenement area, leaving many occupants homeless. Moreover, suitable trees are so widely scattered that considerable time must be spent traveling from them to a likely source of food and back again. Thistle's vast den under the house had none of these drawbacks, and a number of advantages. It was sheltered from the wind. It was roomy and comfortable, and safe. Nesting material was plentiful and, being just overhead, very easy to obtain. So was food. It was produced simply by making a racket at the back door, and waiting for it to open. So when the housewarming party finally broke up around dawn, practically none of the guests departed.

While the festivities still had been in progress, several of those in attendance had given Thistle an important lesson in survival. Never, never choose to live in a place that has only one means of escape. A tree dweller should make sure that at least one other grows close enough to the den tree to permit swift departure, if need be, along its contiguous branches. In a cave such as Thistle's, possible invasion by a predator or any other menace made a second means of egress imperative. This was taken care of when the guests removed several more stones from the foundation on the other side of the house, and for good measure they also opened up a tunnel next to the back door, to make begging for handouts more convenient.

Since raccoons seem to have stomachs with no bottoms, those handouts weren't anywhere near sufficient to sustain the entire mob. And since raccoons are averse to expending energy, except in squabbling with each other, the search for other edibles consisted mainly of digging for grubs and worms, a pursuit engaged in so relentlessly that by midsummer the grounds all around the house looked like a minefield, pockmarked by so many craters that walking through it became an adventure in precise navigation.

As a member of the mob, Thistle was forced to join in this search for edibles, but she had one great advantage over the others that she fell back on more and more frequently as worms and grubs became harder to find. She was well acquainted with the little swinging door as a means of getting into the house, having gone through it many times in her days of companionship with Chowder. She was also adept at opening cabinet doors. Her raids were swiftly executed, usually during the day when her friends were asleep under the house, sometimes snoring so that I could hear them through the floorboards.

If I caught her in the act of pilfering, she would gallop madly away, plunge through the little door, and whisk into the tunnel. But at intervals of fifteen minutes or so she would make additional attempts, until she hit upon a time when I happened to be elsewhere. Then she would snatch whatever was available, a bag of cookies, a box of oatmeal, crackers, or even a dish of cat food. Once I arrived on the scene just in time to see a whole loaf of bread departing through the swinging door. Encumbered with it as she was, Thistle made an astonishingly swift getaway, and my pursuit ended abruptly as the loaf of bread slid into the tunnel, just ahead of my hand reaching out to grab it. Soon afterward there were sounds of bickering and thumping under the house, indicating that the others had awakened and were demanding their share of the prize.

Raccoons are not true hibernators, but in colder climates they're supposed to sleep through most of the winter, subsisting on the fat their bodies accumulated during the fall. Perhaps living under a warm house made these raccoons different, or perhaps Thistle was responsible for the unorthodox behavior. Anyway, she and her friends stayed awake and, although certainly fat enough, perpetually hungry. Since they could hear me moving about up above as well as I could hear them down below, my footsteps going toward the back door gave them ample time to emerge before I did, and when I opened the door they would all be lined up, beseeching with outstretched hands.

Buying food for them as well as for a large population of birds and squirrels became such a financial problem that I cut expenses by buying bags of flour and turning the house into a miniature bakery. Then toward the middle of February, when the temperature was well below freezing and it seemed any sensible animal would want to remain dormant, there was almost explosive activity under and in the immediate vicinity of the house, wails and snarls and shrieks and growls that sounded as though war had broken out and the raccoons were either murdering each other or being murdered. I listened with misgivings, knowing only too well what that meant. In two months there would be a lot of raccoon babies, and more bottomless stomachs to fill.

One morning a neighbor telephoned to warn me not to be taken aback when I went into the barn, that they'd left an injured raccoon in it. Evidently hit by a car, the raccoon had lain on the main road, helpless and whimpering, all through the night and the following morning, with cars whizzing by and people walking past, and no one trying to help it, until the neighbor and her son asked for a cardboard box in one of the stores, lifted the raccoon into it, and then, not knowing what else to do, brought it to the barn.

There it lay, the biggest and most beautiful raccoon I'd ever seen, in what looked like excellent physical condition, wearing a fine coat of rich dark brown fur. One of her forelegs was broken. Her nose was broken and bleeding. And all along one side of her body, patches of clotted blood showed that there were wounds beneath the fur. She couldn't lift her head, but her eyes looking up at me seemed to beg for mercy.

There wasn't much I could do. I brought out a bowl of warm water and put my hand under her head to lift it up so she could drink a little. Then after a while I went out again with another bowl full of warm bread and milk, not really expecting to find her alive, but she was still breathing, noisily and laboriously. When I held up her head it bobbled erratically, but to my surprise she managed to suck up some of the bread and milk.

The next morning, I entered the barn reluctantly, almost certain that I would find a cold, lifeless body, but as soon as the door was open I could hear her breathing, air whistling rapidly through the broken nose. I spoke to her, and when she looked up at me there was no longer fear in her eyes, but a softness of expression that I chose to interpret as gratitude. I still had to hold her head, but she drank warm water and ate some of the bread and milk with a show of enthusiasm.

The broken leg looked as though it was in good enough position so that if it were just left alone it might heal without too much deformity. The nose had stopped bleeding, and she had managed to clean it a little with her tongue. I ran my fingers through her fur and found that most of the wounds had dried nicely and were beginning to form scabs. It began to look as though there might be some hope for her, but all too often I had seen animals I'd thought were well on the way to recovery suddenly expire from internal injuries. She had eliminated nothing, and that was a bad sign.

The following morning there was partial reassurance. The lower part of her body was soaking wet. I dried her with a towel, pulled the wet hay from under her body, and tucked in dry bedding as best I could, and she lifted her head a little and whimpered. Then she ate all of the bread and milk I'd brought, and a bit of cat food, too. But she still was not out of danger. Damage to her intestines remained a possibility.

However, the morning after that, I could smell her even before I opened the barn door, and the lower part of her body was an awful mess. After she had eaten I brought out a pan of water, a washcloth, and a towel, and gave her a sponge bath. She didn't seem to mind, even when I shoved the cloth between her legs to wash her belly. When she was finally clean and rubbed fairly dry with the towel, I lifted her a little to slip clean bedding under her, and all at once I heard a sound that puzzled me for a moment, a low rumbling keeping time with the whistling of air through her nose. She was purring.

From then on recovery was swift. I didn't have to hold her head any longer. She was able to sit up and eat by herself. And finally one morning when I opened the door I found her standing, her mouth open a little as if she were laughing. She promptly fell down and I worried for a moment about the broken leg, but she pulled herself back on her feet and even took a few tottering steps over to meet me, her eyes on the dish in my hand.

Then came the morning when she was no longer in the barn. I called to her and hunted for her, and finally noticed that someone had dug a tunnel under the sill to get into the barn. She couldn't have done that herself, but the excavation was large enough to permit her exit. Just outside, in the light dusting of snow that had fallen during the night, I discovered a pathway of raccoon tracks going between the barn and the tunnel under the house. Since it was most unlikely that she had done all that walking, I deduced that she must have had a number of visitors.

That evening she was with the mob at the back door, limping and a bit unsteady on her feet, but when I tossed her a slice of bread she caught it nicely, and managed to hold her own in the turmoil while she ate it. Apparently she had been accepted by the family and was living with them, for she appeared with them nightly from then on. But she hadn't forgotten the barn. A while later I found evidence that she had gone back there, perhaps often. In the mound of hay, in the precise spot where she had lain when I had nursed her back to health, there were two tiny, naked, newborn baby raccoons. They were dead.

Soon after that, one by one the other raccoons failed to appear at the back door in the evening. Yet the mound of bread I left near their tunnel was always gone the next time I looked. Then I began to hear strange sounds under the house, something like a motor running, I thought, or cats purring, only quite a bit louder, and all at once I remembered the two babies I had found in the barn. Under the house there were some others, healthy, lively, purring, and kneading the fur on their mothers' bellies with tiny hands that because they were naked looked exactly like a human's. And I understood the absence of beggars at the back door. Newborn babies were too precious to be left untended. Food had to be snatched up in a hurry and carried to the nest for consumption.

But eventually preoccupation with motherhood waned, and members of the tribe gathered once again outside the back door, their bellies all caved in, nipples bare of fur and swollen with milk. And a few weeks after their return I was startled by what sounded something like a flock of birds chirping outside, traveling here and there but seeming to concentrate and intensify near the back door. Puzzled, I hurried to open the door, and a lot of little balls of fur, rotund raccoon babies suddenly silenced, stared at me in horrified disbelief before diving out of sight, back into the tunnel.

After a few more brief encounters, however, the babies came to identify me as the purveyor of food, of awesome size but benevolent, the equivalent, you might say, of mankind's conception of God. Then confidence begat impudence, and they squeezed between their elders, crawled under their bellies and climbed over their backs, to try to scale my legs and snatch at the omnipotent hand that did the dispensing. The short-tempered mothers, driven to distraction by their constant chattering and milling about, growled in warning, then struck out to send the youngsters sprawling, but with the resilience of youth they picked themselves up and came right back, only to be repulsed again.

An accurate count of the unruly mob was impossible, but after many tries I settled on an approximation of fifteen, which so impressed me that I bought larger quantities of flour and increased the bread-making to three or four loaves a day. Then toward the middle of the summer I saw in the midst of all the pushing and shoving an alien figure, not chunky like the raccoons but slight of build and delicate; not brown, but black and white. It didn't seem to mind being buffeted about, and the raccoons didn't seem to mind its presence. Mostly it was just ignored, while it calmly maneuvered around to pick up bits of bread wherever it could, sometimes from under the very nose of a momentarily distracted matron. When it was established as a nightly visitor, I tried chucking slices of bread to it, and sometimes my aim was good enough so that it was able to catch the bread before somebody else did, and so it became aware of my presence.

That was how we became acquainted, Jake and I. He was not, however, my first skunk friend.

3

It was long before the advent of the raccoons, in the early years when I stayed in the country only during the summer and returned to the city in the fall, that I first encountered a skunk. This particular year was a lonely one, in which I was unencumbered by even a single cat, and since my needs were few I had a somewhat involved way of obtaining groceries. I ordered what I wanted by telephone, the grocer had the order ready for my neighbors to pick up when they returned from work, and I went down to the neighbors' house to carry it home. That was why I was always away for a while around sundown.

It had become my custom to leave in front of the house a "whoever plate," containing leftovers and scraps for anyone that might be hungry. Usually this attracted nothing but flies during the day, but someone must have taken note of my departure in late afternoon, because the dish was always empty when I returned home. Occasionally I would catch a glimpse of something unidentifiable hastily departing as I approached. My guess was that the visitor was a dog or a cat. Quite possibly it was a raccoon, awakened and made bold by hunger, but I knew little about raccoons then, and nothing at all about the animal I found at the plate one evening, except that it had a terrible reputation and was to be avoided at all costs.

Mostly black, with a white stripe down each side of its body, long fur, and a plumy tail tipped with white, it was so beautiful that I'd certainly have tried to make friends with it, had I not known what it was. When it became aware of my presence the tail jerked up, but it went on calmly eating, taking dainty bites and chewing a long time, while I stood clutching the bag of groceries, not daring to move, afraid even to shift weight from one foot to the other, until finally, after having nosed all around under the plate to make sure not a single crumb was left, the skunk slowly ambled away.

At the same time the next afternoon, exactly the same scene was enacted. I came home and found the skunk at the plate, and stood motionless, waiting until it finished eating and departed. The afternoon after that, the plate was already empty and the skunk was sitting on the steps, barring entrance to the house. As I approached, it made no effort to run away but, in fact, did just the opposite. As it advanced toward me I started walking backward, then broke into a run, going along one side of the house, around the back, and up the other side. The skunk followed, but I gained on it enough to dash up the steps and into the house, and with the door safely closed behind me gasped with relief. What was the matter with the skunk? Could it be rabid?

The fourth afternoon the skunk, looking quite normal, again was sitting on the steps. Again we played tag around the house and I fled up the steps. The fifth day it finally dawned on me that the skunk bore me no ill will but was just hungry. Either someone else had consumed the food on the plate or there hadn't been enough to quell its appetite. Cautiously I approached and eased my way up the steps. Nothing happened. Cautiously I emerged from the house again with a slice of bread, an offering that was graciously accepted and carried a little way off to be consumed.

So we became friends. I'd return home with my bag of groceries and say, "I beg your pardon. May I get into the house, please?" and the skunk would move a little to one side to make room for my entrance. I'd come out again, at first with just a couple of slices of bread, then with cookies because I discovered they were much preferred, and finally, each day, a can of cat food that was eagerly devoured, the tin licked clean and the hand that held it sniffed carefully to make sure no trace of food remained there.

This pleasant interval was enjoyed every day until the weather turned cold and the time came for me to return to the city. On the last day I left a great heap of food on the steps, hoping that my friend would put on enough fat to get through the winter safely. Whether it did or not I never knew. There was no sign of it the following spring.

My second encounter with a skunk was far from pleasant. One day a young girl came to me begging for help. Her brothers had set a leg-hold trap in the swamp down the road, and the skunk they'd caught had been lying there for two days because nobody had the courage to go near it. She led me down through the swamp and across a clearing, to where a group of boys stood staring at a small heap of black and white fur some distance away. Was the skunk still alive? One of the boys nodded. It moved a little when they yelled at it.

An old trapper once had told me that he'd let many a skunk out of his traps. "They seem to know you're trying to help them," he had said. "You just have to move easy, and keep on talking. For some reason, they like the sound of the human voice."

Slowly I walked across the field, and started talking as I neared the skunk. The trap had closed on one of the back legs, high up, near the hip. Kneeling down, I touched the trap, and with agony in its eyes the skunk followed the movement. Because I couldn't think of anything else to say, I kept repeating, "Don't be afraid. I'm trying to help you. Don't be afraid. I'm trying to help you." The jaws of the trap were rusty, so hard to pry apart that it took all my strength, but slowly they started to give and the skunk squirmed, feeling an easing of the pressure. Then suddenly the jaws snapped all the way open. The skunk jerked in momentary fright, lay still for a moment, and started easing away. Out of the corner of my eye I saw the girl coming across the field to join me, and the boys loping away, no doubt disappointed and somewhat embarrassed by the anticlimax they had witnessed. The skunk started dragging itself over the ground, too badly injured to walk, and the girl began to cry.

"Take it home," she begged.

There was a limit to a skunk's tolerance. I tried to tell her that, but my success in releasing the miserable creature had been proof that I was invulnerable.

"Take it home," she pleaded. "It will die if we leave it here."

We were walking along in the same direction the skunk was taking. It clawed its way over the ground more and more slowly, and finally seemed to run out of strength to go on. The girl was right. It would die if we just left it there in the middle of the field. I bent over it, thinking that if I made two swift moves simultaneously, seizing it by the scruff of the neck with my right hand while I pressed the tail down with my left, I might be able to pick it up.

I wasn't fast enough. One hand caught hold of the skunk all right, but the other failed to stop the tail from flicking up, and even in its weakened state the skunk aimed perfectly, sending a jet of yellow liquid over its back and straight into my eyes.

I thought I would die. I wanted to die. My eyes were on fire. My brain was on fire. My head was exploding. My whole body shook. Water streamed copiously from my eyes and my nose.

The girl pulled a handkerchief from my pocket to wipe my face, then said, "Here, blow," as if taking care of her littlest brother. With a hand clutching my arm to guide me, she led me out of the field and out of the swamp, and as I stumbled along blindly I became aware of the body cradled in my arms. Somehow, in that fraction of a second, even while the skunk was spraying, I had managed to pick it up.

By the time we arrived home I could see a little, although through tears, and both of us had stopped gagging, but the odor was still strong enough, as it would be for several days, to make the girl unwelcome at the dinner table when she got home.

In a large cardboard box we made a bed of hay,

and with some trepidation I lowered the skunk onto it. The tail stayed limp and the body lay as I placed it, almost as if it were no longer alive, but the eyes were alert, following our movements. At one end of the box we lined up three bowls, one with water, one with milk, and the third containing some cat food. When I checked the next morning I found the level of the water lower, indicating that some of it had been drunk, but the milk and the food hadn't been touched. The skunk's injured leg was horribly bloated, and purple with gangrene. When I bent over and put out a hand it only growled feebly, without moving. Two days later, it died.

For a few weeks after that, the girl reported, the boys refrained from trapping. But that was as long as the penance lasted.

Now here was my third and much happier encounter, with a little stoic named Jake, who didn't mind getting jostled about by the raccoons, or being hit in the face with a badly aimed piece of bread. Night after night he came to dinner along with the raccoons, and when the weather was bad he came without them.

The raccoons didn't like to go abroad in the rain. Jake apparently didn't mind. With his long fur plastered down, so that his slight body seemed dwindled to almost nothing, he'd calmly shuffle around in a downpour, gorging on whatever appealed to him in the mound of food hastily tossed out the back door, while under the house the raccoons, made even more crotchety than usual by the inclement weather, bickered and fought, perhaps blaming each other for the rain.

When summer gave way to autumn, raccoon attendance fell off for another reason. Beechnuts and elderberries had ripened and were plentiful, and were much preferred to bread. Sometimes one or two of the gang would show up, sometimes none at all, and again, for no reason that I could determine, the whole lot of them would be back. Whichever way it was, Jake remained constant, and on those nights when all the raccoons were absent we became good friends. Instead of bread I'd give him cookies, or pieces of meat that he accepted from my hand with the utmost courtesy, never snatching, taking care not to graze my fingers with his sharp teeth. Begging for more, he'd sit up, with forepaws neatly turned down, thus putting his only means of defense temporarily out of operation.

After we'd had a few heavy frosts the raccoons became faithful again. Jake was shoved out of the way and had to be content with whatever bread he could pick up, but that lasted only until the first snowfall. The raccoons disliked snow even more than rain. As soon as an inch or so lay on the ground there was no evidence of them except for a line of tracks that went from their tunnel to the brook and back again. Each night this same route was traveled until there was a well-worn pathway, and when finally we had deep snow, that turned into a trough.

For a while longer Jake's pudgy little tracks wandered around, making erratic designs in the snow, and he continued to greet me at the usual hour. But after a really heavy fall of several feet, he failed to appear, and from then on I opened the back door to confront a white silence, and walked in solitude where I had ploughed through such turmoil. The only visual proof that the raccoons were still in residence was the deepening trough leading to the brook. Even though there was now only a faint gurgle of water running under thick ice, so that the trip back and forth surely must have been purposeless, it continued to be made nightly, like a ritual that had to be performed. Each night I put out bread near the back door and sometimes it disappeared, but most often it was still there in the morning, with bird traceries all around, and squirrel tracks converging on it from every direction. There was, however, audible assurance that the raccoons still existed. Whenever I went into the room under which the crawl space narrowed, I would hear every once in a while the deep rumble of someone snoring.

The winter was fierce, bitter cold, with winds gusting up to seventy miles an hour. Keeping water pipes from freezing became a constant preoccupation, day and night, and a crisis finally came when the drain froze, so that there was no way to get the water running into the house out again, except laboriously by the bucketful.

Once more, as on similar occasions in past winters, I thought wistfully of the days when, having escaped from the big cities where all my early years had been spent, I plunged into the freedom of rural life with a total renunciation of modern conveniences. The soft glow of oil lamps and candles illuminated the house. Water was obtained by dipping it out of the brook through a hole cut in the ice; and a visit to the sanitary facility, a small retreat attractively screened by drooping hemlock branches, was anticipated by bundling up in jacket, mittens, cap, and boots, and coasting down a hill.

No fear in those days that a tree falling on electric wires might suddenly immerse the house in inky blackness. No worry about pipes freezing and bursting or the toilet overflowing because the drain was frozen. No need to beg a plumber to exchange his services for the equivalent of a month's supply of groceries. Though admittedly somewhat awkward and time-consuming, that way of life had been blissfully uncomplicated.

Now, having fallen victim to the insidious lures of those conveniences I had eschewed so successfully for a while, I was confronted with all their disadvantages, the most immediate of which was the necessity of thawing out the drainpipe. That required shoveling away snow and chopping ice to free the trapdoor to get into the crawl space, then inching along on hands and knees toward the drainpipe at the far end.

As I slowly made my way through darkness dispelled by an almost played-out flashlight, I heard not a sound other than the rustle of my own passage. Yet I could feel that I was not alone. Crouching, then lying flat on my belly because that was less of a strain, I pressed the hot iron I'd brought in with me against the drainpipe. Then there was nothing to do but wait, with the flashlight turned off to save the batteries, and in the renewed darkness the silence seemed to press against me, heavy with some unseen presence. Snapping the light back on again, I directed the beam toward the corner where the crawl space narrowed, and saw reflecting the light a cluster of eyes, a great many eyes. The raccoons were all there and they were awake, staring at me, but not one of them moved. Muttering an apology for having disturbed them, I turned the light toward a corner on the other side, and picked out a small bundle of black and white fur that I presumed was Jake. Then, to my utter consternation, what I had thought was only a boulder lying next to me slowly quivered alive, and turned into a huge opossum. The little eyes in the broad head stared at me sleepily for a moment, then evidently dismissed me as being not worth bothering about. The head went back down under the belly, and after a few more small adjustments the opossum became a boulder again. Hardly daring to breathe lest I awaken it again, I turned off the light to obliterate my identity, and in the dark waited until a satisfactory gurgle told me that the drain had thawed out. Then cautiously I backed away and eased out of the sanctuary, with a fervent vow never, never to return.

4

CONTRARY TO POPULAR BELIEF, nature is far from infallible. Mistakes are made, and probably one of the worst is the selection of February as the month for most small wild animals to mate. Lured out of safe, warm dens to search for mates in deep snow and killing cold, none but the fit are likely to survive. And on second thought perhaps this is not really a mistake, but just another of nature's ingenious, ruthless schemes to keep populations under control. This particular February made no concessions. The temperature stayed near zero during the day and went considerably below that at night. Almost three feet of snow lay on the ground. Yet each night the customary spring riot took place under the house.

The raccoons wailed and shrieked and growled and yelped, and in their den where the crawl space narrowed there was an almost constant thudding that I finally decided was caused by heads bumping against the floorboards as they wrestled or engaged in whatever antics are part of the mating of raccoons. From a corner over on the other side came even more piercing wails and squeals, accompanied by a stench that slowly seeped up into the house, forcing me to open a window to admit fresh, icy air. Evidently Jake had acquired a mate.

Since even the most dedicated student of animal behavior would be reluctant to pursue this particular avenue of research, I doubt that anyone will ever find out exactly why skunks spray when they mate. Could it be two males battling over the favors of a female? Or does the spraying by the female act upon the male as an aphrodisiac during prenuptual exercises? Or does she discourage him thus, holding him off until her fervor reaches a pitch to match his?

Fortunately the skunks made fairly short work of their connubial orgy. After three nights of what sounded like anything but bliss, they became silent, and the air stopped smoldering. But the raccoons' celebrations continued and became even more raucous, finally spilling out from under the house to continue in the snow, and even up in the trees. Evidently determined to make the most of a diversion enjoyed, if indeed it was, only once a year, they managed to prolong it for almost a month. But at last the area under the house became so quiet that I might have thought they had moved out, if I hadn't once in a while seen a masked head poking out of their tunnel, to stare at me with some animosity until, one appetite having been satiated and recovered from, the other appetite returned, and food placed near the tunnel started disappearing again.

As spring temperatures slowly rose, natives used to say the snow was rotting, a figure of speech that seemed particularly appropriate this time, because the more than three feet of it didn't really melt. It just turned mushy and slowly sank. As soon as the level had gone down sufficiently to make traveling possible, all kinds of tracks appeared. Raccoon handprints, so like humans' in miniature, fanned out in all directions. The more delicate imprints of the skunk, spraddled like those of a waddling old woman, meandered here and there but ended, somewhat mysteriously, at the old barn in back of the house. And one set of starlike indentations, emphasized by exclamation points made by the opossum's naked tail, went purposefully toward the road, across it, and into the woods beyond.

The opossum did not return. Perhaps he had searched for and found a mate, or perhaps he'd simply returned to a summer home he maintained somewhere else. But the raccoon tracks all came back to converge at the tunnel near the back door, while the mystery of the skunk's one-way trip was solved when a huge mound of earth and debris appeared beside the old barn, under which a tunnel had been dug. Apparently Jake had tired of living in such close proximity with the noisy, quarrelsome raccoons, and had made a home of his own nearby. Apparently, too, he was determined to be ahead of them, because in broad daylight, while they were fast asleep and snoring under the house, he would poke his head out of his tunnel, and whenever I went by, his bright black eyes would follow me around, until I made a trip into the house and brought out some bread.

The next step, soon taken, was that instead of just his eyes following me around, all of him emerged to accompany me practically everywhere I went. Soon I became so used to his presence that one day when I was showing some visitors around and they asked, "And what is this little animal following us?" I answered without thinking, "Oh, that's a skunk. He —" and got no further because they all ran as if they were thieves and I'd yelled "Cops!"

That is the sad irony of the skunk's being equipped with those scent glands under his tail instead of tusks or horns on his head, or sharp claws on his feet. He is feared, even hated, when his disposition is only to be friendly.

Toward evening one day, when in the waning light identification was difficult, I thought I saw Jake carrying off a piece of suet that had fallen from the bird feeder. It was the very last piece, and suet was not easy to come by, so I ran after him and made a grab for it, only to realize, while we engaged in a polite tug of war, that the white markings on this skunk were not familiar, and it was not Jake but a total stranger. Nevertheless I hung on, muttering an apology and an explanation that the suet really belonged to the birds, and to my astonishment the skunk let go as if it understood. Triumphantly I returned the prize to the bird feeder, then was overcome with remorse. Such gentlemanly behavior had to be rewarded in some way, I thought, so I went in to explore the refrigerator, and came out again with a good-sized chunk of meat. The skunk was still there, nosing around under the feeder, probably hoping it would come upon the suet a second time, his keen sense of smell telling him that it remained somewhere in the vicinity. "Here," I said. With a little growl that I chose to interpret as "thank you," the skunk took the meat from my hand and scurried off with it.

Toward the end of May, Jake stopped following me around. And just at this time, too, the raccoons failed to meet me at the back door. Their disappearance I understood. They were busy tending to newborn babies under the house. But Jake? In dark moments I suspected the raccoons had driven him away or even done him in, although that was most unlikely, for such a misdeed surely would have fouled the whole neighborhood.

Crouching near his tunnel I called and called, and finally was rewarded with a response. A tousled head poked out, emitting quite menacing whuffing sounds to indicate my presence was not welcome. I took the hint and left, but returned with an offer of food. There was no sign of Jake and he didn't appear again when I called, but a little later I saw that the food was gone, plate and all. Then some time during the night the plate was returned. In the morning I found it in front of the tunnel, polished clean, and when I put down more food it vanished again.

Was Jake responsible for these disappearances, or someone else? The next day I sat near the plate to keep watch, and soon Jake's head appeared. Giving me a brief, not-too-friendly glance, he took the plate between his teeth and dragged it into the tunnel, and almost immediately I heard strange sounds, something like rats squealing. Was it possible that rats were living under the barn and competing with Jake for the food? Were they attacking him? I rapped on the wall, and the squealing stopped.

For several more days Jake continued to drag the plate out of sight. Then just as he emerged one day he seemed to go through an odd upheaval, and from under his belly some tiny heads peered out, replicas of his own in miniature. He had become a mother!

Growling fiercely, misnamed Jake tried to herd the babies back into the tunnel, but had no success. While one was being shoved in, another was squirming out. Finally she gave up and went to the plate, and six babies swarmed after her. Gathering around the food in a tight group, they snatched and squealed and shoved and gave Jake such competition that she managed to get only a few bites.

The following day I carried out two plates, one for her and one for the babies, but that turned out to be no solution. The babies simply split into two groups, and once again ate most of the food. So the day after that I took out three dishes, put down two for the babies, and from the third fed Jake bits of food by hand. This worked out so well that it was a routine we followed from then on.

Meanwhile the raccoons also had brought forth young, bringing their total to an estimated thirty-five, and nights became so chaotic that I doubted any creature not protected with a pelt as impenetrable as theirs could have survived embroilment in one of their brawls. My own passage among them became increasingly hazardous, and after having one of my legs mistaken for an adversary several times, I took to wearing slacks almost as heavy as their hides. Prudently, Jake and her family became diurnal, remaining under the barn, probably sleeping, all through the tumultuous nights, coming out in the morning, advancing their dinner hour to coincide roughly with my having breakfast, and spending so much time in the afternoon somewhere near me that I almost began to feel like one of the family. Too young to have acquired caution, the youngsters climbed boldly onto my lap, and after some hesitation Jake joined them, to take with the utmost delicacy pieces of dry cat food produced from my pocket.

This was a nice time for the family, when the babies were unaware of the vastness of the world and its hazards, and confident that all of life would be good. But Jake was an astute mother. She began taking them on educational trips, along the banks of the brook, upstream and downstream, and finally all the way to the foot of the hill where the water spread into a large swamp. On these excursions they formed a line, an undulating, snakelike procession, the lead baby tucking its nose under Jake's tail and each of the others tucking its nose, in turn, under a preceding tail. Whenever I saw them starting out I tagged along, partly out of curiosity, partly to be with them in case they ran into any sort of trouble. I never knew whether Jake was aware of my presence and didn't mind, or whether the job of guiding her family was so all-absorbing that I, at the end of the line, became extraneous. With her nose to the ground, her body flat, her tail draped over the lead baby, she snuffled along, solemnly intent, it seemed, on going nowhere, because they never arrived at any destination, until one day when they went down to the swamp, then partway up again. There, as if being slowly swallowed by a large boulder, the whole line disappeared. Under the boulder was an old woodchuck burrow that Jake must have discovered on some previous occasion and remembered.

On their first visit they came out again almost immediately, but on subsequent trips they stayed, and I had to go back up the hill unaccompanied. But always around noon the next day they would be home again, waiting to be fed. No doubt one reason for their absenting themselves was the undesirability of having raccoons as neighbors. In the comparative peace of the swamp and its environs Jake could teach the young ones how to forage for food and thus achieve independence.

There came a time when, instead of having a serpentine appendage trailing after her, she began taking the youngsters down the hill in pairs, making three trips, each time with two noses tucked under her tail. I supposed this had something to do with the various segments of what had been an entity failing to adhere, because not long after that they all went off on their own, although never straying very far from Jake's immediate vicinity.

The first sign that all was not well with the family came when I noticed two of them wandering around blindly, with their eyes pasted shut. Thinking they had somehow acquired a simple infection, I took the little ones on my lap and, while Jake watched anxiously, washed their eyes and put in some ointment. The next day their eyes were pasted shut again, and so were those of the other babies. Taking care of all of them, one after the other, became something like working on an assembly line.

For several days I continued treating the eyes without any success. Then the babies started disappearing. Only four came with Jake one day. The following day, three. Then two. And just at this time I noticed that something was wrong with the raccoons, too. Uncharacteristically subdued, they gathered outside the back door as usual and reached up to take bread from me as usual. But then instead of eating they only fingered the bread and dropped it, gazed up at me with unutterable sadness in their eyes, and silently slipped away.

Nature can't abide surpluses, yet is always creating them, and the various ways of achieving a mean between these two extremes are in themselves extreme. An unwilling witness to the ravages of disease during the all-too-frequent periods of adjustment, I sometimes suspect that surpluses actually are built up so that the pleasures of destruction might be enjoyed. Certainly it would seem that nature's vaunted balance might be attained in a somewhat kindlier, cleaner, and more orderly fashion, without resorting to such brutality, and without such wild fluctuations from overabundance to near extinction. Only toward the end of a destructive orgy is there some evidence of restraint. Seldom is an entire species wiped out.

Of the thirty-five raccoons, two were allowed to survive. One was Thistle, apparently so favored that she remained totally immune to the terrible disease. The other survivor was a half-grown youngster that I presumed was a male, to guarantee the building of another surplus, in time.

But with the skunks, nature evidently became too enthusiastic, or perhaps absentminded. In violation of what I had though to be a hard-and-fast rule, every one of them perished.

Or, as it turned out, all but one.

W HY IS IT THAT ORPHANED ANIMALS are most often found on or near a road? Obviously because they are the ones that are found. Others, less fortunate, are abandoned somewhere in the woods or fields and are doomed to slowly expire, unless discovered and dispatched more mercifully by a predator.

In exactly the same way that Thistle had been rescued earlier, Poppy was found lying in a roadside ditch, a tiny baby skunk, fuzzy furred, soaking wet, and very, very sick.

She couldn't have been brought to us at a worse time. The house was packed with cats. A baby bluejay occupied the front porch, an orphaned squirrel, the back porch. The only territory still left unclaimed was the guest bedroom, and in it, on the bed in a cardboard box filled with hay, Poppy became an unlikely guest.

It seemed impossible that in so tiny a body so many things could be wrong. She was burning with fever, shaking with chills, and soon gave evidence of having a severe case of diarrhea. Under the baby fur her skin was a mass of scabs, and a big fat tick protruded from one ear.

Which should be dealt with first was a problem, but the tick was easiest to eliminate. A touch of iodine killed it, so that it would dry up and fall off in a few days. Then penicillin was given for the chills and fever, Kaopectate for the diarrhea, and the scabs were treated with hand lotion.

A skunk's scent glands are functional soon after birth, so, young as she was, she could have given me a good gassing. But she must have realized I was trying to help her, or else she was too ill to care what happened to her. Without any protest she allowed me to poke in her ear, shove pills down her throat, squirt unpleasant liquid into her mouth, and soak her skin with something that must have smelled terrible to her.

For a few days thereafter she stayed hidden in the hay in the cardboard box, emerging only to use the pan of earth I had provided, or to suck bread and milk from the palm of my hand. But as she gained in strength there were signs of surreptitious activity.

Things started disappearing. A rubber glove I had left on the bed vanished, followed by a handkerchief, a towel, even a small pillow. She had dragged all of this stuff, the pillow certainly with much difficulty, and hidden it under the hay.

Authorities say skunks don't build nests. Living under buildings or in burrows abandoned by other animals, they are content to leave things pretty much as they find them. Poppy set out with zeal to disprove such assertions. Other things I put on the bed were appropriated in short order. Added to the bulging nest were scraps of cloth from my sewing, a piece of string, a whole newspaper, which she thoroughly shredded, an old pair of bedroom slippers, and several spools. But the spools reappeared every once in a while, chased all over the bed by a vastly improved Poppy. She played exactly like a kitten, batting them with her paws, scrambling after them, capturing and hugging them to her belly while she kicked with her hind feet. For further diversion she picked out of her pan of earth small stones and twigs and leaves that also became playthings. So did some bottle caps I gave her and, if left within reach, the bottles themselves.

With this odd assortment of toys she played contentedly by the hour, until she discovered something she liked better. My fingers, being alive and animated, were a lot more fun. Whenever they came near her she would seize them and nibble on them, and her delight if they wriggled sent her into such contortions that she'd end up standing on her head. From then on, all she wanted to do was play the finger game. Her hearing was acute. Long before I reached the door of her room she would know I was coming, and in anticipation of a game would hurry to the edge of the bed to greet me, hopping up and down with such glee that almost always she fell off.

Skunks can neither jump nor climb, so I'd have to pick her up and put her back on the bed, thus giving her a chance to capture the fingers, and also putting ideas in her head. A sure way to get the fingers to play with her was to fall off the bed, which she did with increasing frequency until she was falling off practically all the time. I'd divert her attention to one of her toys long enough for me to make a swift exit from her room, only to hear a plop, sometimes even before I had closed the door. So I'd have to go back to pick her up again, and once more get my fingers entangled in a game.

Just leaving her on the floor didn't solve the problem, because soon she made another discovery. If I didn't come back immediately, the thing to do was make a dreadful noise on the door, scratching it with her claws. That made me return in a hurry.

Obviously, living in solitary splendor in the guest room bored her, but just as obviously I couldn't forsake all other activities to keep her company all the time. Friends who had heard about her advised me to have her descented, so that she could safely be given the freedom of the entire house. The operation was a simple one, illegal in our state, but I could easily slip her across the border to one in which skunks were not protected. I was sitting on a powder keg, the friends warned. Sooner or later something was sure to irk Poppy, and there'd be an explosion.

But I had no intention of keeping Poppy. As soon as she was old enough to take care of herself, we would go walking in the woods, I thought, and she would grow accustomed to living there as Thistle had done. Depriving her of her only means of defense, those scent glands, would make that impossible. For the rest of her life she'd have to be confined, never knowing the joys — and hazards — of freedom, never meeting another skunk, never mating, never bearing young.

Was there an alternative? Did she have to stay imprisoned in the guest room, or did I dare allow her to come into the rest of the house, fully equipped as she was? How would she react to all the comings and goings, the strange sounds, sudden noises? Would she get along with the cats? There was only one, possibly disastrous, way to find out. Try it.

The next time she fell off the bed and started scratching, I opened the door, and left it open. "Come on out," I told her. Then I put on a pair of glasses, just in case, and waited, camera in hand, thinking I might get a rare shot of a skunk's jet being fired, but hoping I wouldn't.

Snorting with uncertainty, Poppy shuffled cautiously out of her room, and with one accord the cats moved from wherever they were to higher ground. From the safety of chairs and table tops and shelves they stared with misgivings at this latest intruder, while she started exploring, circling around the room to snuffle noisily at everything. Except for this sound, and the tapping of her claws on the floor, there was absolute silence.

Finally she came to a cardboard box, left on the floor because blind Marco, who was always given special favors, had taken a liking to it. From the safety of a chair on the other side of the room he listened to the sounds made by this strange creature, whether large or small he had no idea, and when he heard them approaching his box it was more than he could stand. In spite of his blindness, or perhaps because of it, he had to find out what the thing was, and drive it away from his property.

The instant he jumped down from the chair, Poppy's tail shot up, and she went into the peculiar backward and forward dance that is the skunk's warning of an impending salvo. Remembering the time I had been a victim, I felt apprehension oozing from every pore of my body. Marco made a wide circle around the pattering feet of this unknown menace, achieved his objective, slowly eased himself into the cardboard box, and began nervously washing himself. Poppy stopped dancing, but her tail remained up as she went snorting over to him. Their noses touched. Marco hissed mightily, and Poppy scurried away. I started breathing again, and in a reflex action of relief pressed the button on the camera to take a picture of the ceiling.

The next cat to present a challenge was Hooker, so named because the stub of his tail curled around to resemble a hook, was so much like one, in fact, that it was always getting caught on things and gave him no end of trouble. Once I'd even found him hanging upside down from a wire he'd evidently tried to jump over, looking for all the world like an item of laundry pinned to a clothesline.

Although Hooker wasn't particularly impressive in size, he somehow had managed to bully all the other cats into accepting him as boss of the family. But if confronted by something unfamiliar and therefore possibly dangerous he was, like most bullies, a true coward. One day when we were in the woods, we stumbled on the body of a grouse lying on the ground, an enormous bird extending death-stiffened claws in what seemed to be an impending attack.

Hooker took one look, shot straight up in the air as if jolted by electricity, flipped around in midair, and ran for his life.

However, having noted that only a hiss from Marco had intimidated this stranger in the house, he evidently decided to assert his authority. Ever so casually he swaggered over to Poppy, and gave her a cuff on the nose.

Once again I stopped breathing, but Poppy only dodged. Then somehow she must have given out a warning. Although I detected not a trace of odor, Hooker winced and backed away, looking thoroughly cowed, and to make sure he'd learned a lesson Poppy chased him all over the house, until he had sense enough to jump up on a chair.

That was the end of Hooker's dominion. Poppy became the boss of the household, but a benign, even indifferent one most of the time. With her interest focused primarily on me, she gave the cats only peripheral attention, remaining just a mildly concerned spectator when they had one of their spats, and refraining from becoming embroiled even at feeding time. Hunger always made them especially quarrelsome. While I prepared their food they growled, spat, swatted indiscriminately, bumped into Poppy, hopped over her, shoved her aside. Nevertheless, she persisted in joining the mob at my feet, apparently not minding the commotion, actually indulging in a little diversion by playing with a cat's tail, until stopped by a vehement hiss.

Her amiability was extended even to Hooker, who was allowed to do pretty much as he pleased and go where he liked, as long as he stayed off her rug. Why she took such a fancy to one particular rug I don't know, but just as the cardboard box had belonged to Marco, this rug belonged to her, and anyone who dared set foot on it was attacked furiously, with such terrifying snorts and growls that the cats soon learned to make a wide detour around the rug when crossing the room.

Once I played a mean trick on Hooker by putting some of his favorite food in the middle of the rug, to see what would happen. He stared longingly at the dish, swallowed hard, and with a wary glance at Poppy took a hesitant step toward the rug. Then again some sort of a message seemed to pass between them. As if given permission, Hooker walked boldly onto the rug and started eating, while Poppy stood by watching. That lasted until the food was gone. The truce ended and Hooker was driven off the rug, not even allowed to make sure that the dish had been licked clean.

It looked as though Poppy's being given the freedom of the house would present no problems as far as the cats were concerned, but there were many other imponderables. I took care not to slam doors, tried not to clatter silverware in the dishpan, dispensed with the vacuum cleaner (rather happily), winced whenever the telephone rang, and held my breath every time I flushed the toilet. But it soon became evident that Poppy accepted all these household noises as being perfectly normal. Even when I caught a cold and did a lot of coughing and sneezing she remained unperturbed, but the first time I blew my nose she snorted in alarm and ran for cover, perhaps thinking that was my way of hissing at her.

Since baby skunks always closely follow their mothers and I was Poppy's mother, she was right behind me wherever I went, so that if I suddenly reversed direction I was bound to bump into her or trip over her. I stepped on her tail so many times that once when I felt something tugging under my foot I said impatiently, "Well, why don't you *tell* me I'm standing on it?"

Kneeling on the bed, I hopped off to almost squash her flat. I dropped a book on her. She seemed to understand these were accidents, but when a whole plate of food slipped out of my hands, turned upside down, and splattered all over her, I thought, "Now I'll get it." Instead, she calmly ate what appealed to her in the mess, then washed her fur while I washed the floor.

The only time she left me unattended was when she made a quick trip to the back room, where the pans for the cats were located. The door to this room was kept closed, but a small cutout at the bottom allowed a cat to enter any time, swiftly if need be, by simply nudging against the curtains that covered the opening.

It seemed unlikely that Poppy would use this facility, especially since the pans contained no earth but only newspapers. How could she know what they were for? Nor could I expect her to submit to being trained like a cat, allowing me to give her a gentle spanking and carry her to the pan just after, or possibly even during, her misuse of another spot. But it turned out that wasn't necessary. Without even a hint from me she would suddenly veer away from my orbit, hurry into the back room, squat in a pan, ardently scratch exactly like a cat, then carefully wipe her behind on the edge of the pan.

The curtains over the opening never closed properly, so I finally decided to replace them with a little swinging door, over which I spent a considerable amount of labor to make it respond to the slightest nudge in either direction. Some of the cats figured out how to operate the door after a few tries. A couple were totally baffled. I had to shove them through time after time, until finally it dawned on them that all they had to do was push. Poppy comprehended immediately, and slapped in and out as if swinging doors were a part of every skunk's heritage. Nor did big doors baffle her. She just hooked her long claws around them and pulled, or pushed to make them go the other way. This in fact became one of her favorite diversions, popping through the little swinging door and opening and closing big doors. Nothing seemed to give her quite so much pleasure as finding out how something worked, then proving to herself, over and over, that she could make it work.

Life settled into the kind of routine so loved by animals, with the same thing done at the same time every day, varied only by my occasional departures to go shopping. As soon as I became active in the morning she was in attendance, helping me with the bed making by pulling the sheets all askew after I'd got them smooth, standing tall to peer over the edge of the tub while I bathed, snorting unhappily because she couldn't join me, then having great fun while I dressed, holding the pants legs shut so I couldn't get my feet through.

Dishwashing bored her, but she puttered around my feet, patiently waiting for me to finish. The swishing floor mop scared her so that she hid, but when the rugs were put back down she reappeared to gleefully roll up each one, as if getting them ready for the movers to cart away.

Once these chores were finished, we had to have a game. Concealed behind a door with only the tip of her nose showing, she'd leap out to take me by surprise, with her tail straight up and her rump in firing position. That was supposed to make me cry in fright and start to run, which so delighted her that she'd flip over in a somersault. The same game in reverse required me to hide and wait until I heard her tapping claws approaching, then jump out to startle her. In a flash the tail would go up, and down again almost as fast, and to punish me for having given her such a scare, she'd give my slacks a good shaking.

Toward the middle of the afternoon she would be plodding after me practically asleep on her feet. Taking pity on her, I'd carry her into her room and put her down on the bed, and gratefully she would crawl into her nest, to stay there until the time came to supervise the feeding of the cats. While they were washing up after their dinner and I was having mine, she played by herself, confronting imaginary enemies, chasing them from one end of the room to the other, stopping short so abruptly when she reached a wall that she upended in a somersault. But absorbed in play though she seemed to be, she remained alert to all happenings around her. If I shifted a foot or a cat jumped down from a chair, her tail shot up and with lightning speed her rump swiveled toward the sound. If two sounds came simultaneously, the rump rotated from one to the other, so rapidly that I was reminded of a belly dancer.

During my evening session at the typewriter, she

lay draped across my feet, after having untied and removed shoelaces, and following this came the best part of the day, when I lay down to read. Standing upright next to the bed, she sniffled and snorted, asking to be lifted up so she could join me. The cats made a beeline for the same objective, and there was considerable complaining until proper places were found, the cats piled up on either side of me like sandbags, and Poppy burrowed under my head, where she made a fine soft pillow. Soon she would begin humming a little song, so softly and soothingly that I'd start to nod over my book. Then after a period of silence her snoring would rouse both of us. Suddenly wide awake, she would be full of devilment, bounding down the length of me, sending protesting cats off in all directions, shaking the life out of my feet, fortunately encased in slippers, journeying back up to chew on whatever buttons she encountered, pulling my book down, walking over it and up over my face, to snuffle in my ears, nibble on my nose, and grub through my hair. The only way to stop her was to put on the glove.

Actually it was a heavy leather mitt. In the beginning I had used only a thin glove, but each day her teeth seemed to grow longer and sharper, and inflicted more damage. She soon learned what "ouch" meant and at once stopped the assault, but by that time blood had been drawn, and finally I was yelling

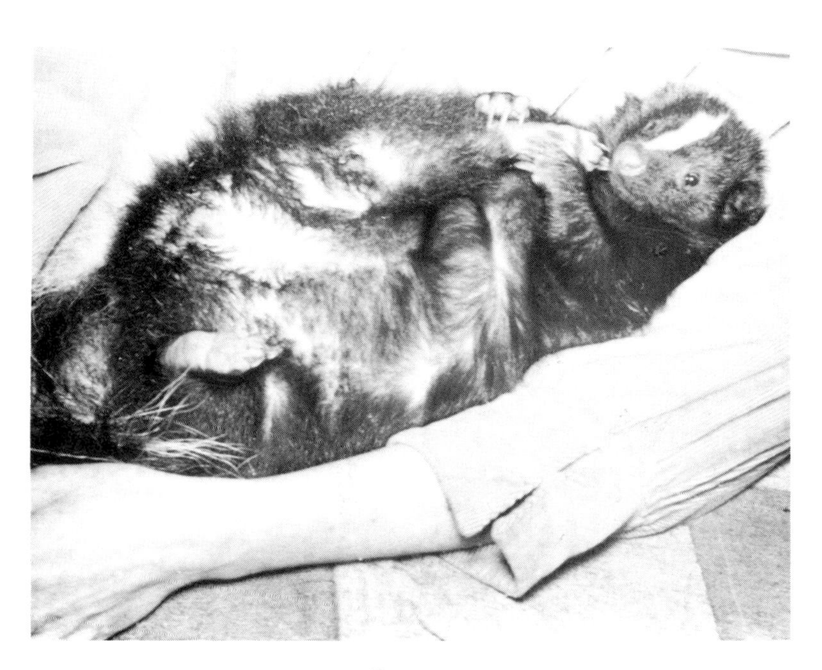

Poppy

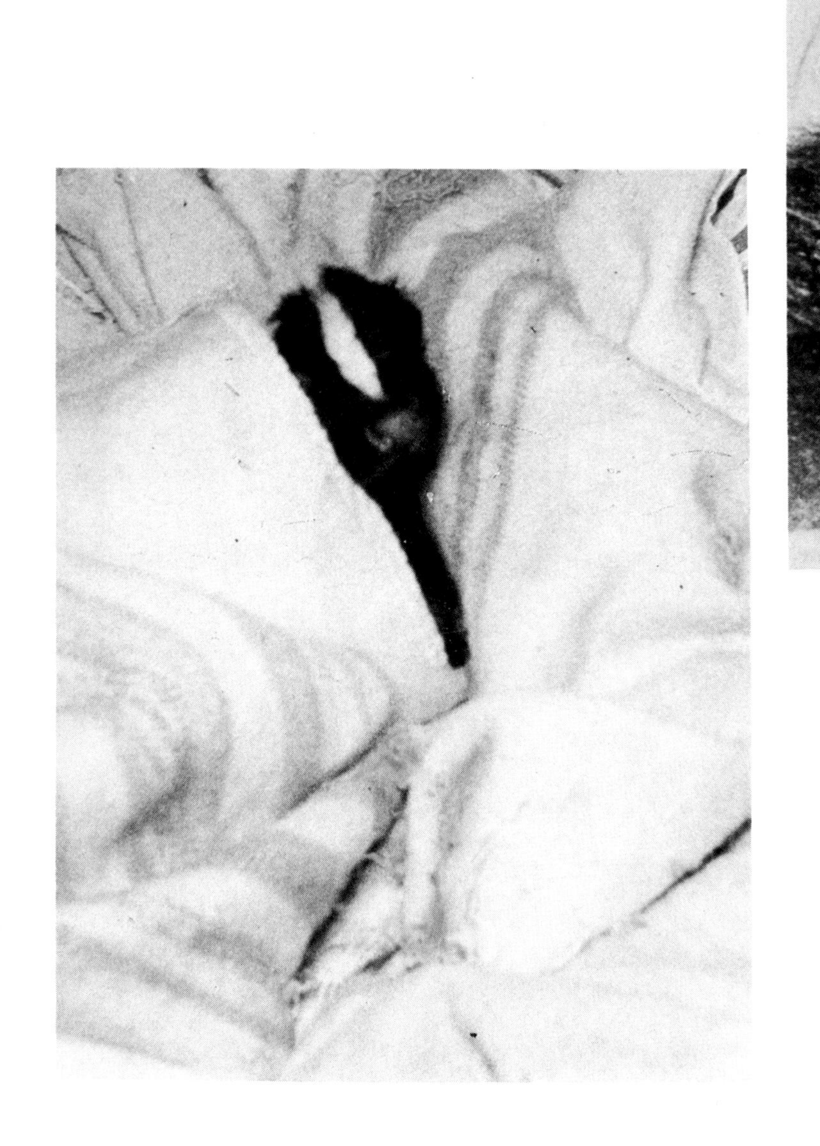

Poppy's first home is the guest-room bed.

When Poppy joins the household, she does not allow Hooker, the boss cat, to step on her rug.

Poppy sits up and begs for what she wants, such as peanuts, or tea in a cup.

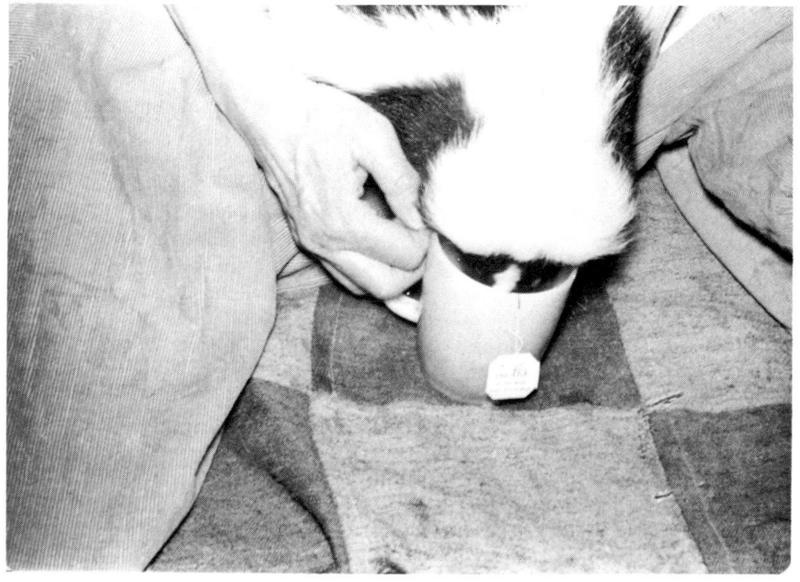

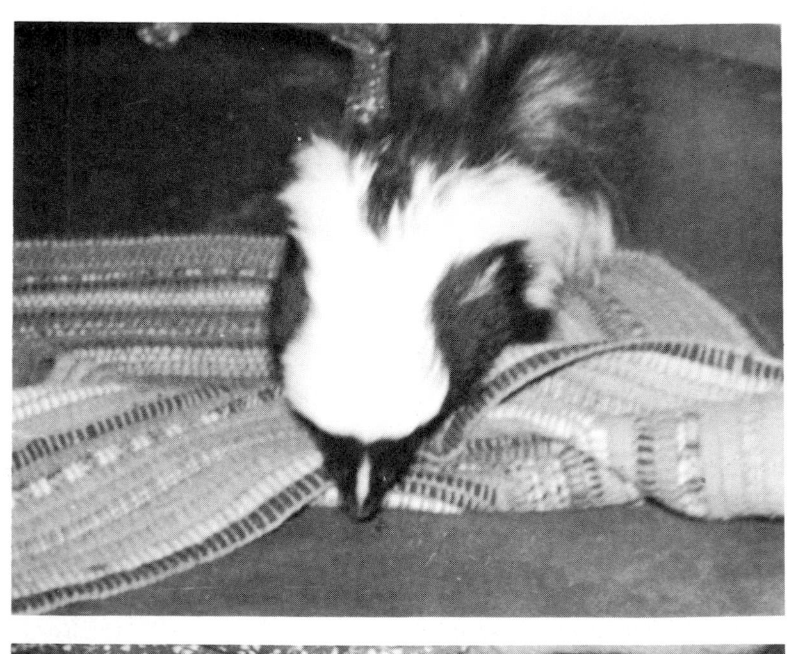

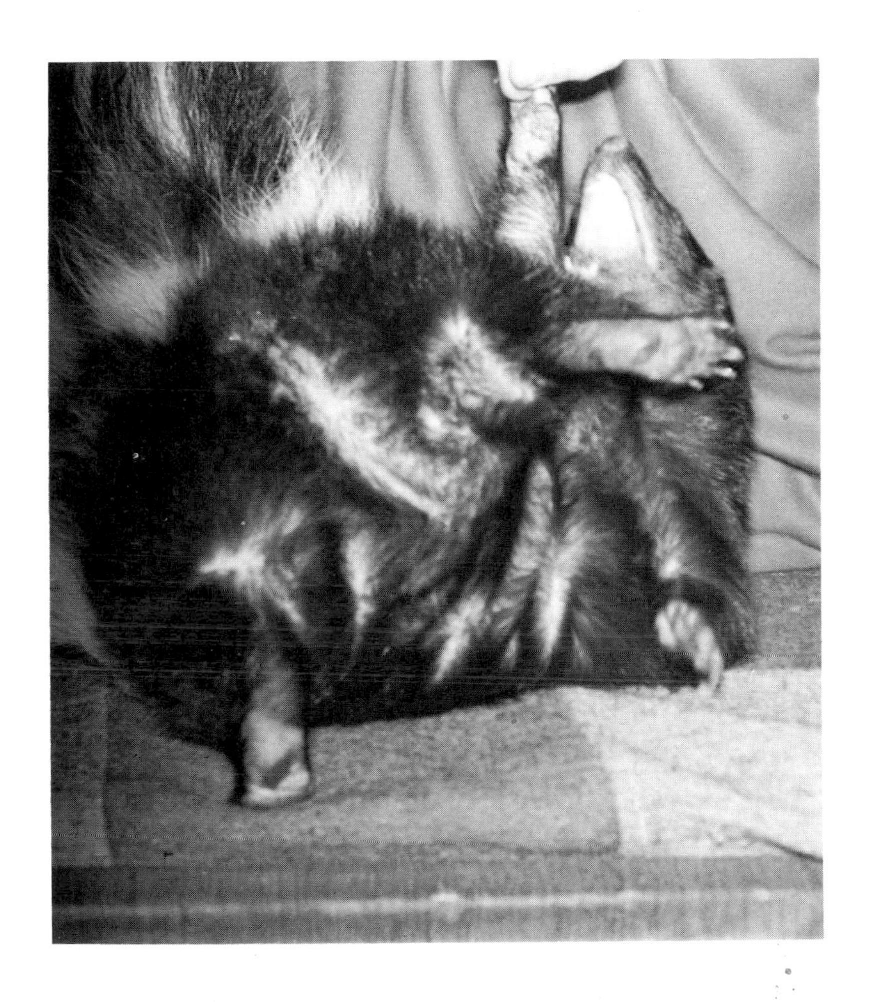

Poppy enjoys rolling up all the rugs, and playing with fingers. She turns somersaults to capture fingers.

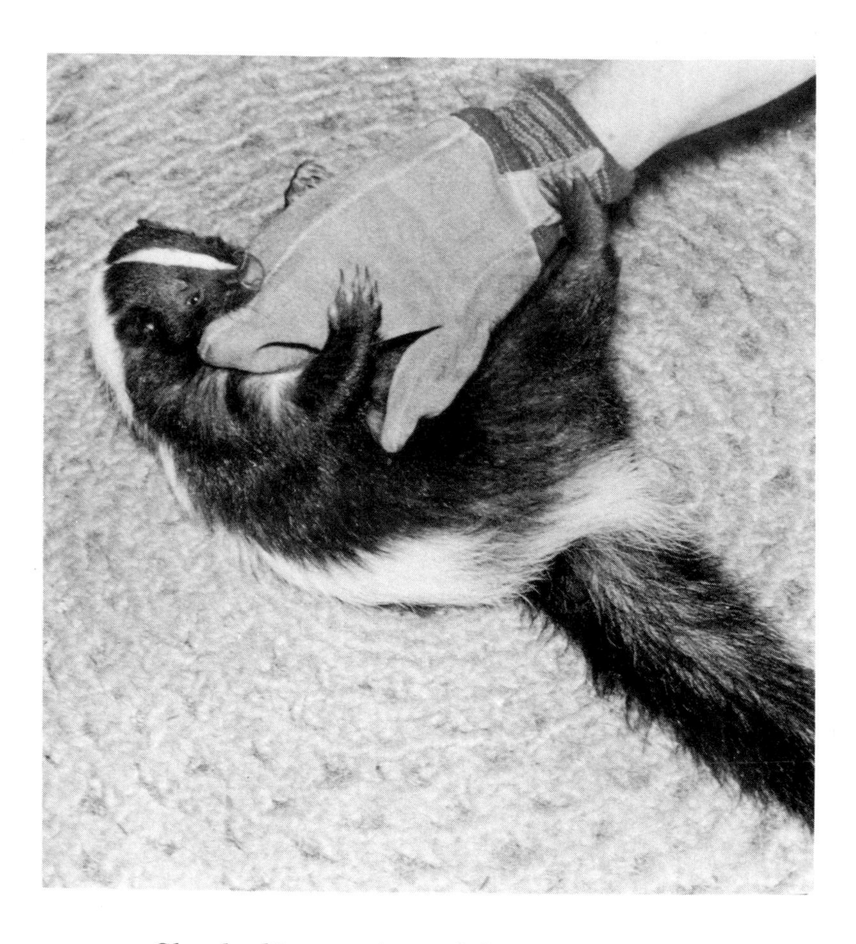

She also likes to seize and slay a leather glove.

When she tires, she burrows under a head and sings herself to sleep.

When she wakes she nips a nose and the owner reacts by inadvertently pushing the cable button on the camera.

Instead of going outdoors, Poppy prefers to play inside with Lowly.

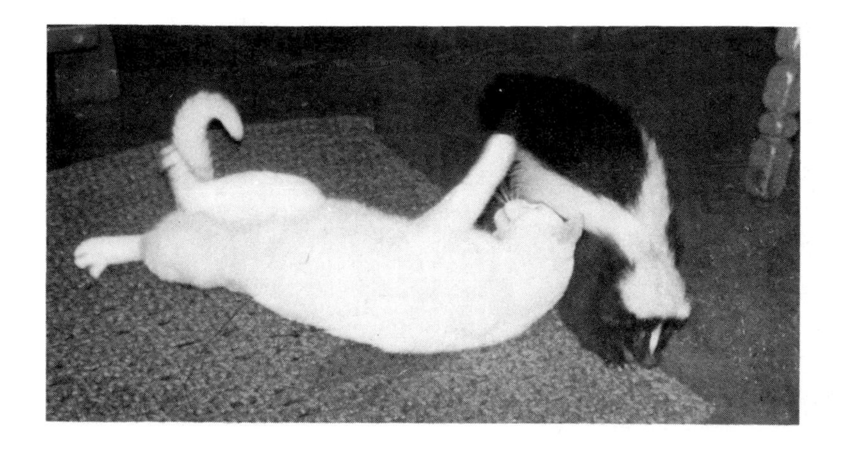

"ouch" so much that the game wasn't fun any more. So we graduated to heavier and heavier gloves, and finally arrived at the heavy mitt.

The moment it was on my hand she would threaten with her rump, her tail so high that the tip touched the back of her head. Then she would attack, in swift darts with an upside-down twist of the head to get at the belly of her quarry, nipping at it and dancing away, tiring it out, until she closed in to tear and shake it to death. From her quicksilver maneuvering, I could see how it was possible for an animal as small and delicately structured as a skunk to dispose of a rat too big for the huskiest of cats to handle.

Having killed the glove, she would ask to be put down on the floor and at once would get on what I came to call her racetrack, which took her under a chair, across the room, under a table, under another chair, and back to the first one, around and around on a course that never varied by so much as an inch, and any cat that happened to be on the track had to get out of the way in a hurry, to avoid being run over.

Going around the track meant she was tired, so I'd say, "Time for bed," and at once she would march to the door of her room, wait for me to open it, march over to the bed, wait for me to lift her up, and crawl into her nest. There she remained sleeping until morning, as far as I knew, although sometimes spools scattered over the bed suggested that she might have got up during the night to have a quiet game.

She always heard me getting up in the morning and was standing at the edge of the bed to greet me, so one morning when she was not there it gave me quite a shock. Had she overslept? I put my hand in her nest and felt around. The little hollow she had fashioned was empty. Had she fallen off the bed during the night? I looked in corners, under chairs, behind a chest. No Poppy.

Bewildered, I stood in the middle of the room and called, "Poppy?" and from somewhere, I couldn't tell just where, there came a short answering snort. Then a slight movement on the bed caught my eye. While I stared at it, a small mound slowly rose, elongated, traveled to the head of the bed, and from under the covers the tip of a black nose emerged, to be followed by a pair of impish black eyes. It seemed Poppy had found a place to sleep more to her liking that the cluttered nest, and from then on she would have nothing more to do with it. Each night she burrowed under the covers.

Contrary to popular belief, skunks don't smell. If made into a coat their fur does have an odor, quite unpleasantly strong if the wearer gets caught in a rain, but this is the smell of death, which seems to last as long as the pelts. When she was still very young, Poppy's glands would react to the excitement of a game and there'd be a trace of musk in the air, but it was far from unpleasant, rather like the scent of new-mown hay. Then as she grew older she gained more control, and unlike most other animals, including man, she seemed to have no body odor at all. The blankets she slept under night after night remained so fresh smelling that I had to change them only once, on the sole occasion when she did lose control.

That was when Mia paid an inappropriate visit.

While Poppy had her afternoon nap her door was kept closed, a needless precaution, really, because the cats showed little inclination to enter the room, excepting, that is, for Mia, who'd evidently got it into her head that, just as the pasture on the other side of a fence looks greener, what was on the other side of a closed door must have special attractions. Possibly this had been on her mind for some time and she'd just been waiting for a good opportunity, because when I went in as usual on this particular day to make sure Poppy had not awakened and fallen off the bed, Mia whisked in right with me, to conduct a quick tour of the room that ended with a leap onto the bed. Probably this would have been all right if she hadn't had a peculiar way of leaping, always aiming at a height considerably above her objective, then sort of falling down upon it. What she fell down on this time, with unhappy precision, was the small mound of Poppy under the blankets, and immediately she shot straight up in the air again, almost to the ceiling. Even in her sleep Poppy's glands had reacted automatically, very likely taking her also by surprise.

Fortunately no great harm was done, even to Mia. All she had got was a bad scare and a lesson she was not likely to forget in a hurry. The bedcovers had contained the odor, keeping it from spreading into the room, and, again contrary to popular belief, the blankets didn't have to be buried or thrown away. All they needed was a good spraying with Lysol and a few days' airing on the clothesline. The only one who really suffered was Poppy. Covered by the blankets, she had given herself a terrible gassing. She washed frantically, trying to rid herself of her very own smell, and for days she had no interest in any kind of food, even peanuts.

Ordinarily she would do anything, including stealing, to get peanuts. In fact, stealing was one of her favorite pastimes. Whenever I couldn't find something, a pen, a glove, a sock, or my sewing, I knew exactly where to look, in the far corner under my bed, and since I was given to mislaying things I actually found this rather convenient, even though it meant crawling into an area not too often visited by a broom. Unlike Thistle, who always demolished whatever she stole, Poppy never damaged anything. A pencil still had a point on one end of it and an eraser on the other. Not a single stitch was ripped out of the sewing, or a pin removed. The only time she ever caused any trouble she was the one who suffered. Stealing a box of chocolates and eating the entire contents, she made herself terribly sick.

What I found somewhat less acceptable was her constant snooping. Whatever I did had to be investigated and, if possible, participated in. I soon learned that I could do no painting while she was around, because if she didn't have her nose under the brush she was sure to have her paws in the paint can. If I took anything off a shelf, a book, a box of paper clips, or some writing paper, I had to show it to her, or she'd try to climb a leg to see for herself. If a package came in the mail she could hardly wait for me to open it, so she could find out what was inside. No matter what door I opened, she had to investigate what was beyond. Over and over she had to discover that the clothes closet smelled of mothballs, the interior of the refrigerator was cold, pots and pans and cans were uninteresting. But one cabinet never failed to arouse her enthusiasm. Whenever I opened its door she hurriedly sat up, because that was where the peanuts were stored.

Sitting up, she had learned, was the one way to wheedle out of me whatever she wanted. So she sat up for peanuts, for candy, for cookies, to ask me to play with her or lift her onto the bed. In fact she almost always seemed to be sitting up, for one reason or another. All I had to do was find out why. If I didn't, she snorted.

Although there is highly audible evidence during the breeding season that skunks are not voiceless, as they are said to be by some naturalists who should know better, they are seldom vocal under any other circumstances. They don't converse, as many other animals do. They don't cry, even when in extreme agony. But they do have some means of communication, one of which is snorting.

A series of short rapid snorts meant Poppy was asking for something. Little sniffles indicated she was pleased. One long snort warned, "Watch out, I'm losing my temper!" This I seldom heard except in the morning, when she was as grumpy before her saucer of apple juice as I was before breakfast coffee.

A skunk also can scare the wits out of you with a fierce growl, but it is seldom used. The only time Poppy gave me a demonstration was when a well-meaning friend sent a gift of a small toy skunk. It was made of plush and certainly didn't smell like a skunk, but must have looked enough like one to convince her that it was a possible rival. When I put it down on the floor her tail shot up, and she backed her rump against it, then let out this growl that sent a chill down my spine. I snatched the intruder away in a hurry, probably just in time, and put it out of view on a shelf.

6

NEEDLESS TO SAY, we had no visitors.

Once word got around that a fully equipped skunk was in residence at our house, people found all kinds of excuses to stay away. Groceries usually delivered at the door were left in the driveway for me to carry in. The man who had promised to come and repair a faulty thermostat became very busy elsewhere. Friends who for one reason or another simply had to see me blew their horns to let me know they were in the driveway a safe distance from the house. Then someone who didn't absolutely have to see me took a chance.

There must be some truth to the claim that women are more courageous than men, because the first person brave enough to confront Poppy was a woman. Moreover, she did so with no great show of bravado.

In an effort to get a good picture, I once walked

without thinking among some totally wild horses, and when I emerged the manager of the zoo nodded with approval. "Good," he said. "You didn't pussyfoot. If you just act like you had every right to be there, they don't seem to mind." I remembered that when the woman came, because she didn't pussyfoot either. She just said hello to Poppy as if it were the most natural thing in the world to pass the time of day with a skunk, and with not the slightest hesitation walked over to a chair and sat down. Somewhat to my relief, and probably hers also, Poppy greeted her most graciously, with her tail carried in a friendly downward curve, then, after some snuffling around her feet, played like a puppy, asking to be petted. But alas, that courageous the woman was not.

Following this initial test, more people flaunted their valor and came to call, and like most animals Poppy showed a distinct preference. Toward women she was invariably cordial, but whenever a man entered the house she ran and hid. I found this not at all displeasing. In fact I'd have preferred it if she had mistrusted women, too, because what she would have to fear most when she returned to the woods was encounters with humans. Willing though she might be to coexist in peace, she was fated to be a pariah because her means of defense was a sickening odor.

From the very beginning she had been free to leave the house if she had wished. In following me around she often had passed the little swinging door that led to the world outside, had observed the cats going through it, even had witnessed with terror the plunging entrance of Thistle on one of her lightning forays. But day after day she showed not the slightest interest in what might lie beyond, and toward the end of the summer, when time for her to adjust was growing short, I realized that the only way to introduce her to the world was to take her into it.

The back door was at ground level, with no steps to confound her. As I went toward it she followed me as usual, then snorted with fear when I opened it and she saw the immensity of the world. But of course she had to go with me. A mother's wisdom was not to be questioned. Since I lacked a tail for her to tuck her nose under, she stayed so close behind my heels that she kept bumping into them.

We traveled slowly along the side of the house, right next to it so she would feel safer, and all went well until three things happened simultaneously. A gang of boys came running down the road, kicking a tin can and shrieking with laughter, a huge truck roaring up the road dropped its entire load of lumber just in front of the house, and Timmy, a great blimp of a sheep who had chosen this inopportune moment to escape from the pasture, rounded the corner of the house to greet us with an obscene belch.

For a moment Poppy stood paralyzed in open-mouthed disbelief. Then she spied one of the raccoon tunnels under the house, dove into it, and that was that. She wouldn't come out again.

This definitely was no way to introduce her to the world. Moreover, if the raccoons woke up, the situation would get even worse. They were bound to resent her presence in their territory, she was bound to react defensively, and the result, seeping into the house, surely would drive us out of it.

I had ceased being the all-knowing mother. She didn't trust me any more. To all my coaxing and pleading she paid not the slightest attention. I put a handful of peanuts at the entrance of the tunnel, knowing that was taking a chance. Although the raccoons could walk past a peanut without seeing it, they had a fair sense of smell and a passion for peanuts that more than matched Poppy's. If they caught only a whiff of these, Poppy would become merely an obstacle to be trampled over.

But even the peanuts didn't lure her out, and with the sun sinking lower and lower in the sky, until it was only a rapidly fading glint coming through the trees, I realized I'd have to do something drastic. Squatting in front of the tunnel, I shoved my arm in as far as it would go, and after a moment felt Poppy's forepaws closing around her old friends, the fingers. I let her play with them for a while, then made a wild grab, hoping to catch hold of the scruff of her neck. Instead I found I had her whole head in my fist.

If ever a skunk had sufficient reason to let go it was then, but she allowed me to drag her out by the head, then hoist her to my shoulder, and we made it into the house just in time, barely managing to close the door against the first of the aroused raccoons.

As soon as I put her down she danced with joy. She was home again! But the good mood didn't last long. Retiring to a corner, she started snorting, big long snorts that meant she was furious about something. I couldn't figure out what, until I noticed that every time she snorted she scratched herself.

The summer had been very dry. For two months we had had no rain, making conditions ideal, I suppose, for fleas. Poppy was loaded with them. Probably the raccoons were, too, but for some reason animals living in the wild seem to tolerate parasites somewhat better than those we have domesticated, and perhaps made less hardy.

Did I dare spray Poppy? When I tried to do the cats they howled as if they were being murdered, and fought with teeth and claws. Would Poppy react the same way and use her weapon? I let her sniff the can and she didn't seem to mind the smell, perhaps because her own could be so much worse. Getting a good hold on her by the scruff of the neck, I took a deep breath, remembered too late that I hadn't put on glasses, hoped fervently that if she did let go she would aim at some other part of me, and pressed the button.

She jerked in surprise as the spray hissed out on her fur and she wriggled to get free, but there were no long snorts, and her tail stayed down. All in all, it went so well that when I rumpled her fur to get the spray down to her skin, she had to turn the whole procedure into a game of catch-the-fingers, ending with a flourish by turning a somersault.

However, the unpleasant introduction to the world had made her wary. Whenever I went anywhere near the back door she made a swift trip in the opposite direction, and hid under the bed. Day after day I tried to lure her out, with peanuts, and chocolate, and fingers skipping ever so enticingly over the floor. Nothing worked. Then the heavy rains of autumn came, and in that steady downpour nobody wanted to go anywhere. The raccoons stayed holed up under the house, the cats stayed holed up inside, and Poppy stayed in bed.

She didn't greet me as usual in the morning, and when I suggested that she get up she only snorted in reply. I gathered together the toys she had scattered over the bed the night before, lifted the blankets, and shoved her saucer of apple juice in so she could sniff it. That woke her up. She yawned and scratched herself sleepily, drank the juice, then as soon as the saucer was licked clean nosed right back under the blankets. All through the rest of the day she slept, and all through the night. Except for the juice, she had nothing to eat or drink.

Such heavy, steady rains used to be called line storms, probably because they almost invariably marked the transition from fall to winter with a sharp drop in temperature. They also marked a drastic change in Poppy's behavior. As soon as the rain ended and the air turned colder, she became active again, but in a most peculiar way.

So that she could get up on the bed by herself, without having to depend upon me to lift her, I had built a sort of ramp, a slanting board covered with a piece of carpet. She had not too much difficulty hauling herself up by digging her claws into the carpet, but whenever she wanted to get down she stood regarding the descent with long preparatory snorts, then made such a wild plunge that she hit bottom standing on her head. Now such tumbles were so frequent that my own head began to ache in sympathy. Up and down the ramp she went, carrying things up to hide them under her blankets. Whatever she could filch that was transportable, a towel, handkerchief, sock, napkin, or even the day's newspaper, if I didn't take care to keep it out of her reach, was whisked off with surprising speed and added to the mound on the bed that kept rising higher and higher. For days this activity absorbed her so that she had time for little else. She ate hastily and sparingly. The feeding of the cats was no longer supervised. She stopped following me around, and didn't burrow under my head any more to sing to me in the evening. All her waking hours were spent dragging things up the ramp. Then abruptly that stopped, and she worked hour after hour pulling on the blankets to tuck them in all around the edges of the mound, until she had fashioned something that looked very much like an Eskimo's igloo.

The first snow fell, and the temperature went all the way down to ten. Poppy crawled into her igloo, and didn't come out again, to eat, or drink, or even use a pan. When I called in an effort to wake her, there was no answering snort. It was almost as if she had ceased to exist. To make sure she was still living I put my hand inside her igloo, into the small round nest at its center. Her body was warm, curled up in a tight ball with the tail covering her head, and she was breathing, slowly but steadily. There was nothing wrong with her. She simply had gone into semihibernation, like her wild relatives in the woods.

For a while the house seemed uncomfortably empty, but gradually we got used to being without her. The cats dozed most of the time near the stove, no doubt relieved that they no longer had to take care not to get caught on her rug or her racetrack. I was busy doing battle with snow and ice and wind during the day and exhausted in the evening. Everything remained quiet and peaceful until the middle of December, when the temperature rose all the way to twenty-five, and we were startled out of somnolence by an almost forgotten, familiar sound. All heads turned to stare at Poppy's door, where a peremptory scratching told us she had awakened and wanted to be let out.

When I opened the door a rumpled, sleepy-eyed, highly suspicious head poked out to look around. Had anything changed while she slept? Cautiously she made a tour of inspection that included checking the identity of each one of the cats. Then she limbered up by taking a few turns around the racetrack, and after that almost exploded into action, hurtling from one end of the room to the other after imaginary enemies, dancing around me, threatening with her rump, yanking out my shoelaces, shaking my slacks, trying to climb my legs.

That stopped when I lay down, and she asked to be lifted so she could join me. Burrowed under my head, she sang her little lullaby, and everything was the same as always, with the exception that she ate nothing. Even her favorites, peanuts and chocolate and cookies, were refused. Nor did she drink anything, or use a pan. It seemed her only reason for emerging from her igloo had been to make sure we were still around, and perhaps get a bit of exercise. When she retired a few hours later she fell into another long sleep. Again she failed to respond to the sound of my voice or the touch of my hand.

It was during this second long sleep of hers that our family acquired another member.

For some time I had been catching an occasional glimpse of something white slipping into the raccoons' tunnel when I opened the back door. To find out what this apparition might be, I put down a plate of canned cat food, checked a little while later, and found the tracks in the snow too ill-defined for positive identification, but the offering seemed to have been taken by either a raccoon or a cat. The next night I put out more food, left the door open just a crack and, bundled up in jacket, cap, and mittens, stood behind it to keep watch. Before long a ghostlike creature approached the plate, a white cat, evidently living in some sort of harmony with the raccoons under the house.

After that I opened the door a little more each night, until I could stand near to the cat and talk to him. Clouds of steam issuing from my mouth probably made me look like a dragon lady, but he didn't seem to fear me. When the food was gone he stood regarding me gravely, as if waiting for an invitation to enter, and upon receiving it he graciously accepted.

Because of his humble origin I called him Lowly, but he turned out to be anything but that in spirit. With his tail carried high he regally ignored the outraged hissing of the resident cats, sauntered across the room like an occupant of long standing, jumped up on the very best chair, hastily vacated by a spitting female, and settled down complacently to wash his face. From then on the chair was his. In fact the whole house was his. An air of complete assurance commanded respect from the others, yet his rule over them was so benign that nobody seemed to mind, even at dinner time.

Then came the legendary January thaw, which in this particular year actually did occur in January, instead of February or March. The temperature climbed to almost forty, and again there was an imperious scratching on Poppy's door. Again she came out looking highly suspicious, made her tour of inspection, limbered up by taking a few turns around the racetrack, and exploded into action, chasing her imaginary enemies. From his chair Lowly watched her antics with awe, then with growing interest, until he could resist temptation no longer. On Poppy's next passage near the chair he soared from it in a great leap and landed on Poppy's tail. I let out a gasp, and so did Poppy. Then, fortunately for all of us, she merely skittered away. With abandon born of inexperience Lowly pursued her, batting the tail from side to side. Around and around the racetrack they went, and so began the strangest of all friendships.

Poppy's tail was ever so much more fun to play with than a paper ball, and chasing after her became Lowly's favorite pastime, second only to eating. He waylaid her on the racetrack to dance over the delightfully feathery tail. He hid under chairs to take her by surprise, stayed concealed behind doors until, unsuspecting, she passed by and he could leap out at her. Sometimes he soared into the air like a ballet dancer and his whole body came down on top of her.

I watched with growing apprehension. How long would Poppy's good humor hold out under such mauling? After all, Lowly would not be the only one to suffer if she lost her temper. But then I began to notice something peculiar. Whenever Poppy passed by a place where she knew perfectly well Lowly was hiding and he did not pounce out on her, she turned around to go past again, and kept on walking back and forth until he did pounce. Or if he lay on the floor just being properly dignified, she would patter around and around him, provocatively brushing his nose with her tail, until he casually reached out a paw to pin her down. It seemed she actually enjoyed being teased.

Sometimes, though, she retaliated and played a trick on him. While he was engrossed in his other pastime, eating, she would sneak up behind him to give his tail a nip. With a gasp he would turn around to hiss, but she would already be somewhere else, looking ever so innocent.

Unfortunately their strange relationship came to an end when the weather turned cold again. Poppy went back into her igloo to sleep some more, and Lowly was left with no diversion but an occasional halfhearted game with a paper ball.

The very worst part of the winter usually comes shortly after the January thaw. This winter was no exception, and I was sure that we'd see no more of Poppy until spring. But early in February, on a bitter cold day, we were startled to hear a persistent scratching on her door.

There was nothing tentative about her entrance this time. She evidently was in a terrible mood. Glaring at me and all the cats, even Lowly, she made a beeline for her racetrack and started running around it at great speed, sometimes even breaking into a gallop. Lowly found it difficult to waylay her and finally was warned to stay away by a fierce snort. Around and around she went, until suddenly she veered off and came over to me to sit up.

Thinking that meant she was hungry after her long fast, I offered everything she liked, peanuts, pecans, raisins, cookies, apple juice, but from each one she turned away in disgust. Back on the track, she raced around some more, again rushed over to me to sit up, and finally I understood. She was begging, not for food, but for my help in coping with a new, most vexing problem. She was in season.

The only solution was, of course, for her to go out and find a mate, but that was impossible. She wouldn't have survived overnight. The temperature was close to zero, the wind was fierce, and the snow was deep. She had never seen even so much as a snowflake. How could she travel any distance, floundering in deep drifts? There was no way out. She simply would have to remain with us during this unpleasant period of unknown duration. But her constant pacing and begging almost drove me mad.

Hour after hour she rushed around the track, hurried to me to sit up, and dashed back to the track again as if she had an urgent appointment to keep. When finally she was so tired that quite literally she couldn't hold her head up and her nose kept bumping on the floor, she would ask to be let into her room, then as soon as the door was closed would start scratching on it, asking to be let out again. The taptapping of her claws on the floor was so constant that I began hearing it even in my dreams.

She also became very dirty, not only physically but in her habits. From the very earliest days she always had been meticulous about using a pan, but now any place would do. Once I caught her starting to squat on my bed, and quite forgetting how she could retaliate if she wished, I seized her by the scruff of the neck to give her a spanking. Fortunately she didn't mind. In fact she acted almost as if she believed the punishment to be justified. Bustling out to the back room, she obediently sat in a pan.

But most annoying of all, even somewhat hazardous, was the way she fell in love with my left arm. From the way it was attacked, hugged, clawed, and raked with sharp teeth, I deduced that skunk lovemaking is anything but placid. I had to be constantly on guard to ward off her onslaughts, and took to wearing a heavy sweater for protection.

This distressing period lasted a little over a month, until the middle of March, then came abruptly to an end. One day she asked to be let into her room and didn't immediately want to come out again. Instead she crawled up the ramp to her bed, nosed into her igloo, and stayed there all through the rest of the day and the following night, and the next morning a brand new Poppy emerged, sparkling clean. Like a drunk taking to the baths after a binge, she must have spent the entire night giving herself a good scrubbing.

Without even a glance at the racetrack, she came to me to sit up, and this time what she wanted was food. She ate and ate, drank some apple juice, and ate still more, as if trying to make up all at once for the long months of fasting. Then she asked to be lifted up, and, settled in the crook of my arm, which had become just an arm again, she washed her face.

This was lovely and even, in a strange way, moving to watch. Putting her hands together and folding the long fingers as if in prayer, she moistened them with her pink tongue and passed them, still folded, over one side of her face, and the other side, then over the top of her head. This took some time, but when at last she was satisfied that cleanliness had been attained in this area, she tended to the rest of her grooming. With pudgy legs thrust out at all angles she washed her belly, and combed with her claws the long fur on the sides and back. Finally she sighed, lay on her back in spread-eagle contentment, and hummed her gentle evening song.

The time for games had passed. The little hoyden had grown up.

7

IN SPITE OF THE COLD and the snow, survivors of the previous year's plague managed to journey from their homes in the woods to celebrate the rite of spring with Thistle. And again her superior accommodations enticed a number of them into remaining. So once again the crawl space under the house was well populated, very noisily for a while, then, as participants slept off their orgy, in deep silence. Only an occasional brief explosion of disagreement told me someone was still living there. Food placed near their tunnel disappeared each night, but I never had so much as a glimpse of the takers.

Finally the snow melted and the air warmed, and the period in which the raccoons probably were busy with their accouchements seemed like a good time to make another effort to convince Poppy that she, too, was a wild animal, who belonged in their environment, not in ours. Like them she was supposed to be nocturnal, but living with us had accustomed her to sleeping at night and remaining active during the day. What we had to do, then, was get her turned around somehow, and the best way to do this, I thought, was to take her for a walk each night until she elected to go out by herself.

Walking during the evening surely would be more peaceful, with no roaring trucks on the road, no noisy children, no sounds at all but the rustling of the night wind in the trees, and no encounters to frighten her. Since I hadn't seen the raccoons in such a long time, the possibility of running into them never entered my head.

Nor did I anticipate having difficulty with the cats. But when we went toward the door on this chosen evening, Lowly suddenly decided to resume his pursuit of Poppy's tail, and my efforts to dissuade him, while coaxing Poppy to stay with me, attracted all the other cats to what looked like a good chance to get outside. So the situation was already complicated when I opened the door, to find on the other side of it Thistle and any number of her friends. She immediately plunged in, her emboldened companions followed, the startled cats tried to leap over them, and in the ensuing confusion, a whirlpool of spitting cats and snorting raccoons, Poppy disappeared completely.

Plunging a hand down in among all the bodies, I managed to locate hers, scooped her up, and hauled her out, probably just in time, and with her clinging desperately to my shoulder, I got everyone sorted out, the raccoons herded in one direction, the cats back in the other. But that put an end to my walking with Poppy on that or any other night. Once again she refused to go anywhere near the back door.

After some ineffectual pleading, I came to the conclusion that the only way left to introduce her to the world was to carry her out, and to avoid another encounter with the raccoons this had best be done during the day. So one afternoon I picked her up, put her on my shoulder, walked out while she snorted long and loud in protest, and a short distance away from the house sat down on the ground. For a while she continued to clutch my shoulder, with her nose buried under my chin, but gradually curiosity took over. Slowly, with diminishing snorts, she crawled off me, and this time we were lucky. Nothing happened to frighten her. To have something to do I raked some of the previous fall's accumulation of leaves into a pile, and she puttered nearby, mostly digging small holes in the ground, for what purpose she probably didn't know. Even if she had unearthed a bug or a worm she would have disdained it, after having enjoyed for so long such delicacies as peanuts and pecans and raisins and apple juice.

From then on I carried her out each day, always going a few steps farther away from the house. Once we came to the edge of the woods, I thought, she would tire of doing not much of anything and perhaps go off for a bit of exploring. But day after day she stayed close, keeping a wary eye on my movements, and the moment I headed toward the house she came bustling along behind me. Then, back in the house, she would go through her little dance of joy because she was home again.

The outings never seemed to give her any pleasure, but were merely patiently endured for as long as I decreed they should last. But I still had hopes that somehow she would become the wild animal she was supposed to be, that like Thistle she might come for handouts and otherwise be free.

One afternoon while we were outside, the telephone rang, and hurrying in to answer it I inadvertently let the door slam shut behind me. The call turned out to be unimportant, just a friend wanting to gossip for a while, and I cut it short, explaining that Poppy was outside and I didn't want to leave her alone. The conversation couldn't have lasted even five minutes, yet in that very short period of time a great deal had happened in the yard.

It was full of raccoons. Why they had awakened and come out in the middle of the day I couldn't imagine, but there they were, milling about, and rushing over the minute I appeared, to beg for food as usual. There was no sign of Poppy, and I never saw her again.

Only months later did I find out, quite by accident, what had happened to her.

During the previous year a large tract of land on the other side of the road had been sold, the trees cut, the ground leveled by bulldozers, and all through the summer it had been filled with campers, trailers, tents, and, of course, people. I hated this campsite and always looked the other way in passing by, but one day the owner hailed me and we stood talking for a while.

They were having a lot of trouble with animals, he said, chiefly with raccoons who raided the grounds at night, stole food from the campers, and overturned garbage cans, leaving messes for him to clean up in the morning. Then, he said, they had had quite a time with a skunk a while back. Appearing in broad daylight, it had strolled around in the campsite, bold as you please, almost as if it thought it owned the place.

Poppy, I thought.

It had to be Poppy. Driven out of the yard by the raccoons, she'd probably wandered across the road, perhaps attracted by the sound of human voices. She liked people, had no reason to fear them. She might even have thought one of the voices was mine, that she would find me there.

The owner had been alarmed by the sound of people screaming, and when he hurried toward the sound to find out what was wrong had seen the darnedest sight, he said, a group of the campers running to get away from a skunk, and the skunk running right after them.

Yes, that was a game we'd always played. She would take me by surprise, I'd pretend to be scared and run, and she'd have great fun chasing me.

The owner had had sense enough not to shoot her, knowing the smell would have made the campsite uninhabitable for days or even weeks. Instead he had set a box trap, and to his astonishment the skunk had walked into it as soon as it was put down.

Yes, she dearly loved boxes, could hardly wait for me to open them, so she could see what was inside.

Imprisoned in the trap, she had been taken for a ride and released "way off somewhere," the man couldn't remember just where. But even if he had remembered, what chance would there have been of finding one small skunk in the vast woods after so much time had elapsed? How far might she not have traveled from that place, wherever it was, in an effort to get back home?

The following winter was a severe one, with deep snow and no respite from the bitter cold even in a brief January thaw. Had she managed to find enough food to tide her over a long sleep, she who had been served such delicacies as nuts and raisins and cookies, with apple juice for breakfast? Had she found a proper shelter, she who had slept in an igloo of blankets in the guest room?

Sometimes I still think I hear the plop telling me she has fallen off the bed, and the peremptory scratching summoning me to open the door for her. And when there is a hint of spring in the air, before Thistle and her friends have emerged from under the house to beg for food, I stand for a while in the early twilight to inhale the faint trace of musk in the air, telling me that somewhere in the woods skunks are mating. Then I close my eyes to bring the memory closer, of those early days when the young hoyden hadn't yet learned to control her glands as she chased fingers and turned somersaults, and there was that trace of musk in the house, a pleasant smell, like new-mown hay. I remember how at just this time of year she had sat up, begging me to solve the problem she could not comprehend, and how for a time she had become enamored of my left arm. Then I send my thoughts into the woods, and hope that somewhere, perhaps far, far away, she has survived and found a mate, and soon will be raising some little hoydens of her own.